Bankers' Securities
A Practical and Legal Guide

Bankers' Securities
A Practical and Legal Guide

Vaumini Amin FCIB, BA(Hons)

First published in 1994

BANKERS BOOKS LIMITED
c/o The Chartered Institute of Bankers
10 Lombard Street
London EC3V 9AS

CIB publications are published by The Chartered Institute of Bankers, a non-profit making, registered educational charity, and are distributed exclusively by Bankers Books Limited which is a wholly-owned subsidiary of The Chartered Institute of Bankers.

British Library Cataloguing-in-Publication Data
A catalogue record for this book is available from the British Library.

ISBN 0 85297 351 9

Typeset in 10/12 pt Times, by Kerrypress Ltd, Luton, Beds
Printed by Stephen Austin & Sons Ltd, Hertford; on 80 gsm paper; cover on 240 gsm

Contents

Table of Cases

Table of Statutes

Table of Statutory Instruments

Preface

The aims of this book are to:

- combine the up-to-date law and practice of securities;
- serve as a practical guide for managers and officers of banks and building societies;
- provide an authoritative source for students taking the CIB Associateship examinations in 'Branch Banking – Law and Practice'.

The book assumes some knowledge of the subject but covers the documents most widely used in practice to a professional level of knowledge and understanding. CIB syllabus requirements are mostly covered.

I have sought to state the law as it stands at the beginning of 1994 and have taken into account the provisions of the Companies Act 1989 and the Law of Property (Miscellaneous Provisions) Act 1989. Although certain sections of the Companies Act 1989, particularly the registration of charges section, have not been in force, they have been included in anticipation that these sections will be adapted or introduced in due course. Every effort has been made to ensure accuracy in the text. However, some errors do occasionally slip through despite exhaustive efforts to provide an error-free text.

Acknowledgements

I acknowledge the kind permission of the following for allowing me to reproduce or adapt certain copyright material:

- Her Majesty's Stationery Office and the Department of Trade and Industry to reproduce material from the Companies Acts and the Insolvency Act 1986.
- Her Majesty's Stationery Office and H M Land Registry to reproduce material from their practice leaflets.
- Northwick Publishers and BPP Publishing Ltd.

Every effort has been made to trace the copyright owners and if any have been inadvertently omitted, an appropriate acknowledgement will be made at the earliest opportunity.

Grateful thanks are due to Geoffrey Reeday for his helpful suggestions and for devoting his valuable time in providing his assistance; Peter Eales for his helpful comments and David Palfreman for all his assistance.

I wish to acknowledge the support and encouragement received from The Chartered Institute of Bankers, especially John Mortimer and Brian Rawle, without whose assistance I would not have had an opportunity to write this book and to Uschi Gubser, Paula Allott and Chris Moon for their assistance.

Finally, and most importantly, I would like to thank my husband, Mahendra, for his support, general forbearance and practical help in proof reading and to my parents Chimanbhai and Hirnaxi Patel, for their constant encouragement; and to them I dedicate this book.

Vaumini Amin
1994

PART I: SECURITIES

1 Security: an introduction

1.1 MEANING OF SECURITY

The term security means the acquisition of rights over property taken to support a borrower's personal undertaking to repay. These rights can be exercised if the borrower (debtor) does not make repayment. An example is a power of sale.

Both real and personal property may be charged to secure the repayment of a debt.

1.2 ATTRIBUTES OF GOOD SECURITY

Security should have a value that is stable and easy to check. The value should be at least that of the advance but, usually, a sufficient margin is required, especially where the value can fluctuate, as is the case with shares. Checking the title and charging of the security should not be too costly and complicated.

The security should command a ready market and be easy to realise. Besides the attributes of specific types of security, property over which a legal charge is taken is usually easier to realise than that covered by an equitable charge.

1.3 THIRD-PARTY SECURITY

When someone else lodges security for facilities given to a borrower, this is known as taking third party security or collateral security.

The advantage of third-party security is that it gives the bank completely separate rights against the debtor and the surety (as the third party is known). If the debtor will not pay, the bank can sue the debtor and threaten insolvency proceedings. If the debtor cannot pay, the bank can prove for the debt in the insolvency proceedings, receiving whatever dividend is finally paid. The important point, however, is that the bank's action against the debtor does not affect its rights against the security taken from the surety. These are still available to the bank. Thus, the bank is able to recover its money from two sources, independently or in combination.

Third-party security can take one of three forms:

(a) a *guarantee*, which involves only a personal obligation;

(b) a *third-party mortgage*, where the third party (the surety) charges property as security for the customer's indebtedness;

(c) a *supported guarantee*, which combines both of the above, the bank acquiring a personal right against the guarantor under the guarantee and an action against the property under the charge.

Technically, there is little difference between the second and third forms above except where an unlimited guarantee is taken. Bank guarantees are 'all monies' securities (*see* Chapter 3), but usually contain an actual limit on the guarantor's liability. Under an unlimited guarantee, the guarantor is liable for the principal debtor's borrowing, whatever the amount, to the full extent of their personal wealth. Under a third-party mortgage, the mortgagor is only liable to the value of the property charged.

1.4 TAKING SECURITY FROM PRIVATE INDIVIDUALS

The following sections apply to all customers, but are particularly relevant when taking security from private individuals. Generally, private individuals are in a weaker position *vis-à-vis* their bank and have less understanding of security arrangements than trading customers. Trading customers are also more likely to have professional advisers.

1.4.1 Undue influence

Where one party to a contract is subject to the dominant position of the other, undue influence can arise. If it is proved, it renders the contract voidable at the option of the weaker party, and the contract may be rescinded (set aside) by the court.

In certain, well-defined relationships, known as fiduciary relationships, a dominant position is presumed to exist, for example, between solicitor and client, doctor and patient, and parent and child. In other relationships, the dominant position must be established by the party wishing to avoid a contract for undue influence (the banker–customer relationship falls into this latter category).

A contract will only be set aside for undue influence where:

(a) the weaker party was subject to the dominance of the stronger party; and

(b) they suffered a real and obvious disadvantage as a result.

It is usual banking practice to insist that a person providing security, particularly a third-party surety such as a relative of the borrower, obtains independent legal advice on the nature of and the obligations incurred under the charge before executing it, and further, that it is executed in the presence of the adviser. This practice is designed to prevent a subsequent plea of undue influence when the bank seeks to enforce the security.

1.4.2 Misrepresentation

Misrepresentation occurs where one party to a contract is misled by the other as to the true facts of the situation – fraudulently, negligently or innocently – with the result that they enter into the contract.

Misrepresentation could affect any contract a bank enters into with any customer, from the opening of a current account to taking property into safe custody. In practice, however, it is most likely to be relevant when security is taken, the customer later arguing that the bank misled them as to the true facts or the legal effects of the charge forms. The misrepresentation may be committed by either the bank or its agent.

In *Barclays Bank plc* v *O'Brien* [1992], the House of Lords held that a creditor will be taken to have constructive notice of the wife's right to set aside the transaction in view of the emotional bond of trust and confidence between a husband and wife when a wife offers to stand surety for her husbands debts and the transaction is not to her disadvantage, unless the creditor takes reasonable steps to satisfy that the wife is warned of the amount of potential liability and of the risks involved and advises the surety to take independent legal advice.

It is clear that no general duty to explain a security document is owed to a provider of security who is not a customer of the bank: *O'Hara* v *Allied Irish Banks Ltd* [1985].

The position is not clear when the security is provided by a personal customer of the bank. *Obiter dicta* (persuasive rather than binding statements of legal principle by a judge) in *Cornish* v *Midland Bank plc* [1985] suggests that such a duty may exist when third-party security (a guarantee) is taken. The duty was recognised in relation to direct security by the High Court in *Midland Bank plc* v *Perry* [1988]. However, in *Barclays Bank plc* v *Khaira* [1992], the High Court held that a bank owed no duty of care in tort or contract to offer explanations or to advise the taking of independent advice to those who came to its premises (customers or non-customers) to sign securities. The court further held, however, that if an explanation is given, the bank is under a duty not to advise negligently on the effect of the documentation and to ensure that it is reasonably accurate. If such a duty is held to exist, its breach entitles the customer to sue the bank in negligence for damages although the security remains valid.

1.4.3   Execution of documents and charge forms

All documents and mortgage forms must be executed in accordance with the provisions of s. 1 of the Law of Property (Miscellaneous Provisions) Act 1989. This section abolished the requirement for a deed to be sealed by an individual.

According to this section a deed must be in writing, and signed and witnessed by at least one person who attests the signature. If it is signed by someone else on his or her behalf (s. 1(3)(a)(ii)), the person signing must do so at the direction of and in presence of the individual and in the presence of two witnesses, both of whom must attest the signature.

In view of the provisions of s. 2 of the Law of Property (Miscellaneous Provisions) Act 1989, it is advisable for the mortgage to be also signed by an authorised bank official.

For execution of all documents and charge forms, the general procedure outlined in Chapter 3 should be followed. The consequences of undue influence or misrepresentation must be considered at the time of execution of the charge forms and documents. An opportunity to seek independent legal advice, especially to a non-owner spouse securing liabilities of the other (third) party, must be given: *Lloyds Bank Ltd* v *Bundy* [1975]. Important cases relating to undue influence and misrepresentation include: *Barclays Bank plc* v *O'Brien* [1992]; *CIBC Mortgages plc* v *Pitt and Another* [1993]; *National Westminster Bank plc* v *Morgan* [1985] and *Bank of Credit and Commerce International SA* v *Aboody* [1989].

1.5   STANDARD CLAUSES IN BANKS' CHARGE FORMS

The standard clauses found in most of the banks' charge forms are:
1. 'All monies' – whole debt clause.
2. Continuing security clause.
3. Consideration clause.
4. Joint and several liability clause.
5. Personal covenant to repay clause.
6. Monies due on service of demand clause and monies due on demand.
7. Conclusive evidence, i.e. any written statement by a bank official informing the customer of the amount due will be conclusive evidence of that amount in any legal proceedings.
8. Agreement regarding power of sale, i.e. after the demand has been made on the mortgagor.
9. Protection in case the bank fails to break the account to avoid the rule in *Clayton's* case operating to its detriment.
10. Amalgamation clause where security effectively passes to bank's successor in case of amalgamation.

11.   Change in constitution of parties – principal debtor or guarantor to be liable notwithstanding such change.

12.   Right of lien and set off, giving the bank the right of lien over any monies belonging to the chargor or any articles or items held in the safe custody and a right of set off in respect of credit balances held to the customer's order.

13.   Additional security clause – security is stated to be in addition to and not in substitution of any other security held.

14.   *Ultra vires* clause – security to be valid even if the borrower is acting beyond his authority.

15.   Right to release, vary the security held or grant accommodation to the debtor.

16.   A clause preventing a third party chargor competing with the bank in the borrower's insolvency and from taking security from the principal debtor and providing that any security received shall be held in trust for the bank.

17.   Preference clause, dealing with the bank's rights subsequent to the release of security in case the charge is subsequently held to be a preference (and therefore voidable under the Insolvency Act 1986).

18.   Right of retention for a certain period of third party security after release.

19.   Beneficial ownership clause – the mortgagor confirms that he is the beneficial owner of the securities charged and does not hold them as as a trustee.

2 Stocks and shares

Legal and equitable charges of marketable securities can both be created without the customer having to execute a memorandum of deposit (legal charge by way of transfer of shares in the banks' name and equitable charge by a simple deposit of shares with the bank), but in practice banks obtain a signed memorandum of deposit so that they can rely on the protective clauses in the charge form. The memorandum also prevents the customer later arguing that the certificates were deposited for safe custody and not as security.

2.1 CLAUSES SPECIFIC TO THE MEMORANDUM OF DEPOSIT

Agreement in respect of bonus shares/dividends or interest paid on shares   The chargor agrees to deposit any bonus or further shares received and pay instalments and meet all calls when they fall due on such shares.

Execute legal transfer of securities   The chargor undertakes to transfer the securities into the bank's or its nominee's name when requested to do so by the bank.

Power of sale   This gives the bank the power of sale over the security at any time after the demand is made.

Power of attorney   Some bank forms include a power of attorney clause covering equitable charges, which enables the bank to create a legal mortgage in its favour, or which appoints the bank as an attorney of the chargor so that the bank, as an attorney, has the power to sell shares without reference to the court for an order for sale.

In such cases, the form must be signed as a deed and the bank must also give the release by deed.

Blank transfer   The chargor agrees to execute a completed, but unstamped, transfer form, which enables the bank to transfer the securities into its own name or that of its nominee company.

Returning the securities   Some bank forms have a clause providing that the chargor will accept equivalent shares (of the same class or denomination). The bank is then not under an obligation to re-transfer the actual shares which were mortgaged.

6

Margin of cover If included and in respect of certain types of facilities, this clause requests the chargor to keep a margin of cover (shares) to protect the bank's position should the value of the shares drop unexpectedly.

2.2 INITIAL SECURITY CONSIDERATIONS

2.2.1 Listed companies

Note: Building society accounts can also be charged by memorandum of deposit.

1. Obtain the share certificate. The name of the owner will be shown on the certificate. Check that the security quoted is in the same form as on the certificate. If the company's name has changed, refer to the *Financial Times*, the Stock Exchange daily official list, or to the broker and amend the name in pencil on the certificate.

If the customer cannot produce the certificate, take care: it could be deposited with another bank as security.

If the certificate has been lost, obtain a duplicate from the company by giving an indemnity to the issuing company for any loss that could be suffered through wrongful issue of the duplicate.

2. Check in the financial press that the value of the security is unlikely to be affected by mergers, acquisitions or capital rearrangement. It is difficult to obtain a realistic value of security for unquoted shares and problems occur when the borrower defaults and security is to be realised. Quoted shares are easily realisable.

Bonus/rights issue: make sure that there are no bonus (scrip) issues in respect of the shares charged so that the shares can be valued at a correct, and not a lower, market price.

Value the shares quoted in the financial press. From the two prices quoted refer to the lower price and then decide the margin that will be required. (This will also depend on the type of shares charged and some of the above considerations.) If the shares are not quoted in the financial press, refer to the latest issue of the Stock Exchange daily official list or a stock broker.

Decide whether or not the bank wishes to take a legal mortgage or an equitable mortgage over the stocks and shares.

Do not confuse the nominal value of loan stock, gilts or local authority holding. Nominal value quotes the amount which will be paid out at maturity or redemption. Until then the market value is an amount for £100 nominal value.

3. For ordinary or preference shares charged:

   (a) Obtain information about the capital structure of the company.

(b)   Bear in mind the investment problems of high-geared ordinary shares which are more speculative if the proportion of preference (fixed interest) capital to total capital is high.

(c)   In hard times, low-geared shares are better. In prosperous times ensure that a higher margin cover is maintained in respect of high-geared shares. Sell them as soon as profits begin to fall, because they normally fall faster than low-geared shares (after demand is made).

4.   Ensure that the shares are not held on trust.
5.   Partly-paid shares. – Do not transfer them into the name of the bank's nominee company. As legal owner the bank is liable for any unpaid amount of outstanding calls, even if the bank has released the shares. If the shareholder fails to pay, the bank will have to pay the liquidator for these calls. It will only have to do this, if the company goes into liquidation within 12 months prior to the presentation of the winding up petition.
    Even if the customer meets the calls, it is possible that repayments.may not be met.
6.   Use the correct charge form, either memorandum of deposit for own account, or memorandum of deposit (third party account), whichever is applicable.
    Most banks have two types of memorandum of deposit forms, one for own borrowing and the other for shares charged by a third party. Some banks also have separate forms for use where only one or two holdings are deposited and it is not likely that any further additions of shares will be deposited; or to cover shares deposited with the bank as security from time to time and where the shareholdings are likely to change frequently.
7.   Charge by a director of the issuing company. Where a bank lends to a director of the issuing company against the security of shares of that company, check that there is no requirement in the articles for a director to hold a minimum number of shares in order to qualify as a director. If such a restriction exists, ensure that the charge does not affect this.
8.   Accuracy of details. – Ensure that the name of the borrower is correctly spelt; the memorandum of deposit is dated; the address for service inserted and all insertions initialled by all the parties to the form. Each page of the form should be initialled by all parties.
9.   Ensure that the bank does not have actual or constructive notice of a prior equitable charge where a legal charge over registered shares in public companies is accepted, otherwise the bank's equitable mortgage will be postponed to the earlier equitable interest. For example, the customer may be a trustee of the

securities and may have charged the security for the borrowing in breach of trust: *Coleman* v *London County and Westminster Bank Ltd* [1916]. It is important to ensure that shares are not held in trust for a club or a society and that a minor does not have a beneficial interest in them, in which case the shares will have been registered in the name of one or more adults or nominees for the minor.

10.   Where shares are offered in joint names, it is good practice to obtain a legal mortgage unless the bank is certain that the parties are not the trustees.

2.2.2   Unlisted (private) companies

1.   Ensure, by checking the articles of association, that the company does not have a lien on its own shares and that there are no other restrictions.

2.   Bear in mind the difficulty of valuing these shares and also the problems the bank may encounter in realising the security. Demand for shares in an unknown company is unlikely to be great. Any restrictions on ownership contained in its articles (see 3 below) must also be borne in mind.

3.   The articles of private companies may impose restrictions on the transfer of its shares and these could prevent the bank from taking a legal charge over them.

Because of problems of valuing the security, realisation, restrictions and transferability, shares in unlisted companies are far from being the ideal security. If they are taken then it is better to retain a higher margin of cover and transfer them into the name of the bank's nominee company in order to strengthen the bank's position.

To ascertain its value, the bank can obtain from the secretary of the company:

(a)   the prices at which the shares have changed hands in the last 12 months;
(b)   information on the dividends paid by the company in the last two to three years;
(c)   a copy of the company's balance sheet for the last two to three years, so that the net value of assets and liabilities can be ascertained.

4.   Use correct charge forms.

5.   Use the standard stock transfer form. The transfer form should be undated, unstamped and signed ('blank transfer') but not registered. Leave address of transferor blank and complete when transfer is registered.

If the bank wishes to register the transfer the same procedure as detailed for listed companies should be followed.

2.2.3   Renounceable allotment letters

The shareholder is sent an allotment letter pending issue of a share certificate and customers sometimes borrow against the security of allotment letters. Allotment letters incorporate a renunciation which must be completed and signed by the allotee, if he wants the shares to be transferred before the date fixed for the registration of shares in his name.

When a company makes a rights issue it will send the allotment letter indicating the number of shares allotted. If the shareholder does not want to take up the rights issue, he can sell the shares by signing the renunciation form so that the shares are transferable as bearer security.

When lending against the security of an allotment letter, check the ownership of the allotment letter, and ascertain the amount which will have to be paid when the instalments are due and before they are fully paid. Read the terms of the letter carefully and ensure all requirements and regulations listed below are complied with.

1.   Obtain the shareholder's signature to the form, the form of renunciation, and his authority to debit his account. Most memorandum of deposit forms have a clause authorising the banks to do this. If appropriate, send the allotment letter for acceptance by due date.

Check that all the shares specified in the allotment letter are fully paid and send the allotment letter for registration in the name of the shareholder or in the name of the bank if it is a legal mortgage.

If the shareholder takes up a rights issue, then the allotment letter is not necessarily required to be lodged. The new share certificate will be sent to the shareholder, in which case ensure that the certificate is obtained from the shareholder.

2.   Deposit the allotment letter at the bank with the memorandum. This enables the bank to sell the shares if the customer does not pay or the bank can also register the shares in the name of its nominee company and acquire a legal mortgage. Most memorandum of deposit forms authorise the bank to sell.

Complete the memorandum of deposit and 'blank transfer'. For execution of the security follow the procedure detailed in 2.3.

3.   If the bank does not intend to take a legal mortgage, obtain the customer's signature to 'blank transfers' provided the transfer is not required to be executed as a deed. When the certificate is issued in the customer's name, the bank can then take the equitable charge, together with power to sell the shares.

4.   For partly-paid allotment letters, first check the allotment letter to ascertain the instalments which will be due on shares before they are fully paid. Obtain the customer's authority to pay them when they fall due and to debit the

customer's account. Also make sure that the box for returning the certificate is completed so that it is returned to the bank.

5. For fully-paid allotment letters, make a diary note for the return of the certificate (if applicable).

6. Use the correct charge forms: either memorandum of deposit (own borrowings) and 'blank transfer'; or memorandum of deposit (third party borrowings) and 'blank transfer'.

Only date the charge form after the last date of renunciation when registration will be effected in the allottee's name.

Use a standard stock transfer form and enter the name of the nominee company on the form if legal mortgage is taken.

2.3 TAKING THE SECURITY

2.3.1 Legal mortgage over registered shares

Although a legal mortgage or an equitable charge can be created without the chargor having to execute a memorandum of deposit (a legal mortgage by transferring the shares into the bank's name and an equitable mortgage by depositing the share certificate), it is good practice to obtain a signed memorandum of deposit for an equitable mortgage: *Harrold* v *Plenty* [1901]. If it is a third party security, a memorandum of deposit must be taken.

After complying with the initial procedure outlined above, the following steps should be taken.

1. Check the share certificate is not a duplicate to ensure that the holding is in the name of the mortgagor, that there is no indication of trust, and that the signature is genuine.

2. Transfer the shares into the bank's name or that of its nominee or nominee company and obtain a blank transfer signed by the registered owner. The name of the bank as transferee should also be entered on this form. Use the correct stock transfer form for each holding.

Make sure that a correct stock transfer form is used (standard stock transfer and not a talisman stock transfer) for signing.

The transfer form should be undated, unstamped and unregistered. Provide the full name and address of the bank nominee company (if undated, do not enter the name of the nominee company). Stock transfer forms are often held undated, unstamped and unregistered until the bank needs to realise the securities.

Even though a bank may have acted in good faith, if a forged transfer is sent for registration the bank has to indemnify the company: *Sheffield Corporation* v *Barclay* [1905]; *Yeung and Another* v *Hongkong and Shanghai Banking Corporation* [1980].

To avoid this problem, particularly where there are joint holders, the bank must ensure that the transferor(s) signs in the presence of the bank official. Send the transfer by post to the second transferor but do not hand it to the transferor who has executed the transfer.

Banks also face problems realising the security when 'blank transfers' are not held. In the absence of 'blank transfers', they have to rely on the customer's co-operation or obtain an order from the court.

If the chargor dies and the company is on notice of his death, without the personal representatives' approval, the company will not register the transfer.

If the bank wishes to register the transfer, send the transfer with the certificates for registration and make sure:

(a) the correct stamp duty is marked;
(b) the description of the shares is entered;
(c) the name and address of the mortgagor as transferor is completed (leave the address of the transferor blank and only complete it when the transfer has to be registered because the address may have changed);
(d) the bank stamp, date and signature in the 'selling brokers' box is completed;
(e) authority from the customer to debit the account is held;
(f) the name and address of the bank's nominee company as transferee is given in the transferee box (Talisman sold transfer forms should not be used).

3. Forward the signed transfer form together with the original share certificate to the issuing company or its registrars. The company will issue a new share certificate in the name of the bank or its nominee company.

4. Complete a memorandum of deposit. Obtain the chargor's authority to debit their account (if a customer) for payment of instalments for allotment letters. If a form covering one or two holdings is used, insert in the schedule details of the holdings. Do not add any more securities after the form is executed (Memorandum of deposit is also used to charge building society share accounts, National Savings Certificates and premium bonds).

If a general form is used in respect of shares deposited with the bank from time to time, do not complete the schedule but record its details in the bank's internal register and change these records when holdings change.

Complete other details of the form, by entering the name and address of the mortgagor or principal debtor, and dating the form on the day it is executed.

5.   After giving the chargor an opportunity to obtain independent legal advice and explaining the principal clauses, obtain a memorandum of deposit signed by the chargor and witnessed by a bank officer or a solicitor. Each page and all deletions and additions must be initialled. The charge form must be executed in accordance with the provisions of the Law of Property (Miscellaneous Provisions) Act 1989.

(a)   Some banks have a standard advice clause typed near the signature section of the forms, so that the person witnessing the signature and giving advice confirms that the contents and implications of the form were explained to the parties signing the form and they confirm having understood the advice. This clause is signed and dated by the bank or the solicitor giving the advice.

(b)   The chargor should sign the independent legal advice clause confirming that he was given an opportunity by the bank to obtain independent legal advice prior to the execution of the documents, but declined to do so and is fully aware of their contents and implications.

(c)   If independent advice is declined, a file note of the interview – with date, time, place, parties and mentioning that independent legal advice was declined – must be made.

If the charge form is to be sent to another bank or solicitor, for execution, follow the procedure in Chapter 3.

6.   Where shares are transferred into the name of a nominee company, keep a record of the dates dividends are to be received and credit them to the correct accounts of the customer (If shares are charged by a third party, credit dividends to a suspense account).Send details of annual reports, balance sheets, etc. to the chargor.

Complete and follow the procedure for the registration of transfer given in 2.2.1.

7.   If bearer shares are taken as a security, retain them with executed memorandum of deposit.

(a)   Even if a memorandum of deposit is not held, if the bank takes up shares under a rights issue, add the cost to the principal sum borrowed (if the chargor is a customer) and to a suspense account in respect of a third party security.

(b)   Make a clear diary note to revalue the shares periodically, at least once a year.

(c)   Make a note of return of share certificate from the issuing company in the name of the bank's nominee company.

(d)   Study the financial press to ensure that any bonus, rights issues, or capital rearrangements will not affect the security charged.

2.3.2   Equitable mortgage over registered shares

When an equitable charge is taken, the shareholder remains the proprietor in the company's records.
1.   Obtain the share certificate in the name of the registered owner.
2.   Value the shares.
3.   Choose a correct form of memorandum of deposit, after enquiring from the customer if only one or two holdings are to be charged, or if shares from time to time will be charged.
4.   Ask the chargor to obtain independent legal advice and also explain the principal clauses of the form. If the mortgage form is sent for execution to another bank or solicitor, follow the procedure in Chapter 3.
5.   Complete the memorandum of deposit. All pages and all insertions and additions must be initialled. The form must then be executed by the chargor with the signature witnessed by a solicitor or a bank officer.

The mere deposit of shares with the bank, with the intention of creating a charge, can amount to an effective equitable charge. But to avoid claims by the holder that certificates are not intended as securities, and to gain the protection of the clauses in the charge, it is good practice to have a memorandum of deposit executed. If equitable charge is taken without the memorandum of deposit, make an interview note to show an intention that they were deposited as a security for the borrowing.

The liabilities of the borrower cannot be secured by a third party by way of deposit of shares without a memorandum of deposit. According to s. 4, Statute of Frauds 1677, there must be written evidence before the bank can enforce the promise.

In *Harrold* v *Plenty* [1901] it was held that the deposit of shares with the intention of creating a charge amounts to an effective equitable mortgage.
6.   Complete the stock transfer form and insert the name of the company, details of the type of holdings and the amount.

The names of the registered holder or transferor should be left blank.

Insert full name and address of the bank nominee company (if undated, do not enter the name of the nominee company).Normally banks obtain a blank transfer (undated and unstamped, but signed by the shareholder) and leave the name of the transferee blank. They insert the name of the purchaser or their own name when the shares are to be sold. In this way the bank will not have to seek the court's permission to sell the shares.

Stock transfer forms are often held undated, unstamped and unregistered until the bank needs to realise the securities.

Even though a bank may have acted in good faith, if a forged transfer is sent for registration, the bank has to indemnify the company: *Sheffield Corporation* v *Barclay* [1905].

Do not date the transfer form, but complete details of shares, name of the mortgagor as transferor, and the names of the bank's nominees as transferee.

Ask the chargor to sign the 'blank transfer'.

7.   A company quoted on the Stock Exchange cannot claim a lien on its fully paid shares and banks do not serve notice if shares fall into this category.

If it is an unquoted company, notice must be given in duplicate to the issuing company or its registrar, informing it that the bank has a charge on the shares and asking it:

(a)   to acknowledge receipt;

(b)   whether it has received notice of prior charges on the securities (although the company will decline to accept the notice it will make a record and advise the bank if transfer for registration is received);.

(c)   whether it has a lien on its shares by virtue of its articles of association or otherwise.

A bank's equitable charge will not be effective if the company, by virtue of its articles of association, has a lien on its own shares, where the shareholder owes money to the company and his debt becomes due after the company received the bank's notice.

In such circumstances, although the company can have priority over receipt of the bank's notice, if it lends further monies to the shareholder after receipt of the notice, it cannot claim priority: *Bradford Banking Co. Ltd* v *Henry Briggs Son & Co. Ltd* [1886].

8.   The issuing company will return the notice with a letter stating that, although it is precluded from noting interest of the bank in its records, it will make a note in its register.

9.   If there is a doubt regarding the mortgagor's integrity, or for some reason it is impossible to take a legal mortgage, a stop notice is served, so that the

company will inform the bank if the transfer is being effected by obtaining a duplicate share certificate: *Rainford* v *James Keith and Blackman Company Ltd* [1905].

To protect against the customer obtaining a duplicate certificate and selling the shares, a stop notice will be served upon the company by filing a sworn affidavit at the Supreme Court, indicating that the bank has an equitable charge. The affidavit and order is then served on the company so that the company has to give the bank eight days' notice of any attempt to transfer the shares by the registered holder. This will allow the bank to obtain, in that period, an injunction from the court restraining the transfer.

This method is followed when the customer fails to repay and the bank is in the process of recovering the monies.

2.3.3 British Government securities

1. Obtain the value from financial press.
2. Follow the procedure in 2.3.4(a)(i)–(iv) and (vi–vii).
3. Make a diary note of the redemption date.
4. If the bank intends to register the transfer in the bank's nominee company, see the procedure outlined in 2.2.1.
5. As stock registered on the National Savings Stock Register cannot be transferred, only an equitable mortgage is possible over it.
6. If the bank wants to strengthen its security by registering the holding in its nominee company, i.e. take a legal mortgage, form GS47G should be used. Until then form GS47G and stock transfer form (signed, undated) are held.
7. As government securities do not attract stamp duty, the reverse of the form (transfer) does not have to be completed.

2.3.4 Unit trusts

It is not possible to create a legal mortgage of the units since the registered holder only has an equitable interest. Therefore the mortgage created must be equitable.

The bank has two options:
(a) The bank should check/ensure:
    (i) the certificate(s) which will specify the number of units held and the registered holder;
    (ii) that a duplicate certificate is not produced and that an indemnity for a lost certificate has not already been issued by the bank;
    (iii) that the unit trusts are still quoted in the same form as when the certificate was issued;

(iv)   there is no evidence of trust;

(v)   they are valued on a nominal amount basis as this will vary from the market price;

(vi)   that the terms of certificate allow transfer or sale to be made by way of stock transfer or other method of discharge;

(vii)   the chargor transfers the units into the name of the bank's nominee company.

(viii)   With the chargor's agreement, obtain a transfer from the managers of the trust, complete it, and send it to the managers with the appropriate registration fees and the chargor's certificate (do not use the Talisman sold transfer form).

(ix)   Diarise for the return of the certificate in favour of the banks.

(x)   When the certificate is received, obtain a correct memorandum of deposit to be executed by the chargor.

(b)   (i)   Obtain the certificate(s) and ask the customer to execute a memorandum of deposit.

(ii)   Obtain the stock transfer form to be completed and signed in blank by the chargor so that the bank can realise, sell or transfer the units when the need arises. Upon the customer's default, obtain his signature to the renunciation (do not date it) which is on the back of the certificate (no transfers are used when units are bought by the managers).

(iii)   Give notice of charge to the managers or the trustees.

(iv)   The managers or trustees will record the notice in the register of unit holders and send an acknowledgment.

2.3.5   National Savings stock registered certifcates

These are government securities. When the stock is purchased, the stockholder's name will be recorded on the National Savings Stock Register. The bonds have a maturity date, but can be encashed on three months' notice prior to the maturity date.

(a)   Follow the same procedure detailed in 2.3.4(a)(i)–(iv).

(b)   If an equitable mortgage is taken, obtain the stock certificate, and the encashment notice from the post office, and ask the customer to sign it.

(c)   Arrange for the memorandum of deposit to be executed. The standard stock transfer form ('blank transfer') should be signed by the chargor.

(d)   To strengthen the security by registering the holding in its nominee company, take a legal mortgage by obtaining form GS47G from the Bonds and Stock Office of the Department of National Savings. When it is registered, the holding will be transferred to the Bank of England Register.

(e)   Make a diary note of the redemption date.

As government securities do not attract stamp duty, the reverse of the stock transfer form does not need to be completed. The Bank of England requires a standard stock transfer form. National Savings registered stock requires the standard stock transfer form GS47G. Form GS47G allows the transfer of stock to the Bank of England Register. The holding remains in the beneficiary's own name. The form should be signed but undated.

Transfer into the Bank of England Register is required because the stock registered on the National Savings Stock Register cannot be transferred, therefore only an equitable mortgage can be created. The bank, to strengthen its security, should use form GS47G and take a legal mortgage.

2.3.6   National Savings Certificates

It is not possible to create a legal mortgage over these certificates. They cannot be transferred into the bank's name, because they are not transferable except in special circumstances, and only with the consent of the Director of Savings.

Banks can obtain an equitable charge by asking the customer to deposit the certificates with or without a memorandum of deposit. In practice banks obtain a signed memorandum of deposit.

Since notice of charge cannot be given to the Director of Savings as he will not accept it, the customer can obtain a duplicate certificate or nominate another person to receive the certificate upon his death. This risk must be considered by the bank.

(a)   Ask for the registered holder's card from which his registration number and signature can be ascertained.

(b)   Check the numbers on the certificates with the details on the holder's registration card.

(c)   Complete the details of the National Savings certificates on the repayment form and ask the depositor to sign the form. Insert the date of purchase and leave it undated.

(d)   If the bank wants to sell or realise the security, date the form and send it with the certificates. The form authorises the Director of Savings to send the moneys direct to the bank.

(e)   Diarise the receipt of moneys.

For premium bonds banks take an equitable charge by:

(a)   obtaining the holder's registration card and ascertaining the holder's number. The holder will not be named on the premium bonds, but the registration number will be quoted;

(b)   taking a deposit of the bonds with the holder signing the repayment form and executing a memorandum of deposit.

Some banks write to the Premium Savings Bond Office (Lytham Street, St Annes, Lancs. FY0 1YN), quoting serial numbers of bonds to check if the depositor is the registered holder.

2.3.7   American and Canadian Securities

Some shares and stock issued by American and Canadian companies are quoted on the Stock Exchange in the UK. The name of the registered holder appears on the face of the certificate. The back of the certificate incorporates a form of transfer and a power of attorney for execution 'in blank' by the registered holder. When signed 'in blank', shares are treated as bearer securities although they are not negotiable by transfer and delivery. The holder, by sending the certificate, can then register his name in the company's records. Most of these shares are registered in 'marking names'.

When these shares are offered as security:

(a)   Refer to a Stock Exchange yearbook which will list the names of firms and stockbrokers or finance houses which are considered as 'good marking names'. Check that the shares offered as security are in good 'marking names'.

(b)   Check the advertisements regularly to see when the dividends are paid so that they can be claimed from the 'marking name'.

(c)   Ask the depositor to sign the memorandum of deposit. The stock exchange transfer form should also be signed 'in blank'. If shares are registered in the bank's nominee company, which is in a 'good marking name', the bank will have a legal mortgage.

19

If stockbrokers deposit certificates with the bank, it is possible that they are holding them in trust for their clients. Provided that there are no unusual circumstances upon which the bank is put on enquiry, the bank will not be affected: *Fuller* v *Glyn Mills Currie & Co.* [1914]

2.3.8 Overseas securities

Procedure for bearer shares and American style securities:

(a)   Obtain the shares and value through the stockbrokers.

(b)   Follow the procedure outlined in 2.3.4(a)(ii) and (iii).

(c)   Check the financial press to ensure that takeovers, mergers, or capital rearrangements will not affect the value of security.

(d)   Use a correct charge form of memorandum of deposit and a stock transfer form (executed 'blank transfer') and arrange for these to be signed.

(e)   Check the Stock Exchange daily official list to ascertain if a standard stock transfer will be applicable, or whether or not a special transfer form has to be used. For special forms, contact the registrar of the issuing company or the Stock Exchange official yearbook.

(f)   If standard stock transfer is required, follow the procedure in 2.2.1.

2.3.9 Bearer securities

If bearer securities are deposited with the bank as security, they may be in the form of bond certificate or share/stock certificate.

Transfer of title to bearer securities takes place by mere delivery as they are negotiable instruments. Therefore a signed stock transfer form is not required.

A bank accepting bearer securities obtains a legal title by delivery provided that it accepts the certificate:

(a)   in good faith, i.e. honestly whether negligently or not: s. 90 Bills of Exchange Act 1882;

(b)   for value, in exchange for something which has a monetary value;

(c)   without notice of a defect in the transferor's title: *London Joint Stock Bank* v *Simmons* [1892], *Lloyds Bank Ltd* v *Swiss Bankverein* [1913], i.e. where it has been obtained without the authority of the true owner.

The formalities as required for registered stocks and shares are avoided, e.g. transferring the securities into a nominee company's name is not required.

Ensure that the bond or certificate is undefaced and correctly stamped and that all unmatured coupons are attached. To claim the interest or dividend, each certificate has a set of coupons attached either with a number or a date. This should be sent for collection on their due dates so that interest or dividends are sent. Make a diary note of the dates the coupons are payable. If dates are advertised, note the number and date of the first due date of the coupon (bearer securities cannot be charged to cover Consumer Credit Act regulated borrowing).

2.4   KEY POINTS TO REMEMBER

Partly-paid shares   Insist on a greater margin of cover than for fully-paid shares, and only lend if the customer is able to meet the calls when they fall due.

Transfer by deed   For stock which is transferable only by deed, do not take blank transfers. Complete the transfer, because an incomplete document which is signed as a deed and delivered, where a material part of it is left blank, is void. Most banks therefore date and complete the transfer when signed.

Equitable mortgage   When taking an equitable mortgage, ensure that there are no other equitable interests in existence. If there are, the bank's equitable mortgage will be postponed to the earlier equitable interest, e.g. if the customer is holding the security as trust: *Coleman* v *London County and Westminster Bank Ltd* [1916]. To protect against this, if shares in joint names are lodged as security, unless the bank is certain that the parties are not trustees, obtain a legal mortgage.

Bonus issues   Always study the financial press to check details of bonus shares issues so that the bank can obtain these shares from the customer, if an equitable charge is taken. If the bank has taken a legal charge, then the correspondence will be sent to the bank. The bank can send it to the customer and ask him to deposit the shares. Some banks' memoranda of deposit have a clause so the chargor undertakes to lodge all future bonus shares as security.

Possible forgeries   Always ensure that the transfer sent to the issuing company for registration is not forged. Otherwise the bank will have to indemnify the company even though it acted in good faith: *Sheffield*

Corporation v *Barclay* [1905], *Yeung and Another* v *Hongkong and Shanghai Banking Corporation* [1980].

Shares in the lending bank as security If customers who are also the shareholders of the bank want to borrow against the security of those shares, check that the memorandum and articles of association do not restrict this. If the bank's articles of association restrict the bank in its lending against the security of its own shares:

(a) ask the customer to lodge the certificate without a memorandum of deposit;

(b) give notice to the bank's registrar.

Lodging of the certificate in this way should only be regarded as evidence of means and should not be considered as effective security.

Private companies If shares in private companies are offered as security, it is preferable to regard them as an evidence of means, because of the difficulties of taking them as security, even though they may be quite valuable.

Shares charged by a limited company The usual procedure for taking a security from a company should be followed (see Chapter 6), i.e. check the memorandum and articles of association and obtain a search on the company (Mortgage Register Search). Obtain a Board Resolution and certified copy authorising the officials of the company to sign the memorandum of deposit. Charges over shares given by limited companies do not require registration at the Companies Registry unless they amount to a floating charge.

2.5   RELEASE OR RE-TRANSFER OF SHARES TO THE CHARGOR

Legal mortgage

1.   Place the memorandum of deposit form to 'obsolete securities'.

2.   To transfer the security from the nominee company into the name of the depositor, the stock transfer form will be used. This must be completed with:

(a)   A full description of the security.

(b)   The consideration money marked.

(c)   The name of the transferor (nominee company).

(d)   The stamp of the branch and date in the 'selling brokers' box.

(e)   The depositor's full name and address.

(f)   On the reverse of the lower half of the transfer form, 'form of certificate where transfer is liable to *ad valorem* stamp duty'. Authorised official should sign against the branch stamp and date which should be the same as the one inserted in the 'selling brokers' box.

3.   Lodge the stock transfer form and the share certificate in the bank's name with the issuing company's registrars.

4.   Diarise the return of the certificate from the company's registrars.

5.   Return the share certificate to the depositor against his acknowledgement of receipt. Do not use Talisman Sold transfer form.

Equitable mortgage

1.   Place the memorandum of deposit to the 'obsolete records' marked cancelled.

2.   Return the share certificate to the depositor and obtain receipt.

2.6   REALISATION

If the customer defaults, make a formal demand before realising the security. If the shares have been charged by a third party, give the third party notice of intent in order to give the opportunity to sell the security at the current market price.

Legal mortgage

For quoted shares:

1.   Obtain stockbroker's opinion if the shares should be sold or be retained in the expectation of a better price (this may result in a fall in the prices in the meantime).

2.   If the bank wishes to sell immediately, instruct the stockbrokers to sell.

3.   If full repayment is adjusted, place the memorandum of deposit marked 'cancelled' with obsolete papers.

Equitable mortgage

1.   Contact the chargor and arrange for the shares to be sold voluntarily.

2.   If the chargor does not co-operate, the power of attorney clause in the memorandum of deposit coupled with an undated but completed stock transfer form, on which it can rely except in case of death, means that the bank will not need to obtain an order for sale from the court to realise and sell the shares.

3.   Sell the shares and realise the proceeds.

4.   Place the memorandum of deposit marked 'cancelled' with obsolete papers.

2.7   MONITORING THE SECURITY

Equitable charge over unquoted shares   It is a good practice to give a notice of charge to the issuing company when an equitable charge over unquoted shares is taken as a security, or where it is likely that the company may have lien on shares (private companies). For fully paid shares quoted on the Stock Exchange a company cannot claim a lien.

Unit trusts   If unit trusts are taken as a security, give notice to the managers or trustees and acknowledgement will be sent.

If the bank is not able to take a legal charge because the shares constitute the customer's qualification shares as a director, it is good practice to take an equitable charge and serve a stop notice.

Allotment letter   When instalment amounts fall due on shares, ensure that they are paid on due dates. Debit the customers' account in accordance with their authority (which should have been obtained when security was taken).

Bearer shares   Make a diary note to send the coupons for collection on the due dates to the issuing companies or their agents and for payment receipt.

If coupons are dated, detach them on due dates and send for collection.

If they are numbered, check the advertisements in the financial press for due dates and only detach when such advertisements appear.

Make sure that a new supply of coupons are ordered from the issuing company or its agents by detaching the 'talon' attached to the certificate and sending it to the company.

Partly-paid shares   Make sure that amounts of outstanding calls are paid on due dates.

Study the financial press to check for announcements, or notices relating to companies, whose shares are charged to ensure that it does not affect the security.

Bonus issues   Check that bonus issues, rights issues, and capital re-arrangements do not affect the security charged.

Valuation of shares and stock   Make a diary note to revalue the holdings every six months or yearly (more frequently if there is not sufficient margin cover).

3 Guarantees

3.1 WHAT IS A GUARANTEE?

A guarantee is a promise to answer 'for the debt, default or miscarriage of another', if that person fails to meet the obligation: Statute of Frauds 1677, s. 4. Primary liability for the debt is incurred by the principal debtor. The guarantor incurs secondary liability, that is, the guarantor becomes liable only if the principal debtor fails to pay. If the principal debtor's liability to the bank is void, the guarantor will not be liable: *Associated Japanese Bank (International) Ltd* v *Crédit du Nord SA* [1988].

A guarantee must be evidenced by a written note or memorandum signed by the guarantors or their agent. Without such written evidence, a guarantee is unenforceable. Bank guarantees are, of course, always written contracts.

In these two respects, a guarantee differs from an indemnity. An indemnity imposes direct or primary liability to pay and need not be evidenced in writing: *Mountstephen* v *Lakeman* [1871].

Bank guarantee forms are, in fact, dual purpose documents. They operate as guarantees where the borrowing is enforceable against the principal debtor – the guarantor by definition incurring secondary liability – but as indemnities where it is not.

3.2 ATTRIBUTES OF GUARANTEES AS SECURITY

3.2.1 Advantages

(a) An unsupported guarantee is a very simple security to take – no registration is involved and no complications concerning proof of title arise.

(b) A guarantee can easily and immediately be enforced by court action.

(c) As with any other security given by a third party (collateral security), it can be ignored when claiming against the principal debtor.

(d) As several parties can guarantee a loan, it is useful security where the principal debtor is unable to provide security but offers a viable business loan proposition.

3.2.2 Disadvantages

(a)   Unless supported by a cash deposit or other security, a guarantee is always of an uncertain value as a security. A guarantor's financial position can change very quickly. An unsupported guarantee should only be accepted after careful investigation into the proposed guarantor's financial circumstances.

(b)   Court action may be necessary to realise the security and a technicality may defeat the bank's claim. For example, special rules apply to guarantees taken from partnerships and companies. A defeat of the bank's claim on a legal technicality would almost certainly be the result of carelessness when taking the security.

(c)   Enforcing a guarantee may cause bad feeling, particularly if the guarantor is a valued customer.

(d)   Litigation may be necessary to enforce payment where the guarantee was not supported by other (realisable) security.

Types of guarantee

(a)   *Specific guarantee:* the guarantor's liability to a particular transaction between the debtor and the bank is limited to a specific sum.

(b)   *Continuing guarantees of a limited amount:* the guarantor guarantees the debtor's liability to the bank for a specified sum, thus limiting his own liability. If possible, banks usually obtain a continuing guarantee.

3.3   GENERAL CONSIDERATIONS

3.3.1   Undue influence

The basis of undue influence

Ensure that the guarantor is not unduly influenced by the bank or, more likely, by the principal debtor, to sign the guarantee. If undue influence is proved, the guarantee may be set aside by the court: *Davies* v *London and Provincial Marine Insurance Co.* [1878]; *Lloyds Bank Ltd* v *Bundy* [1975]; *Bank of Credit and Commerce International SA* v *Aboody* [1989]; *Woodstead Finance Ltd* v *Petrou* [1985]; *Goldsworthy* v *Brickell* [1987].

Proof of domination alone is not sufficient. The guarantor must also have suffered a real detriment as a result of executing the guarantee: *National Westminster Bank plc* v *Morgan* [1985]. The guarantee will not be set aside on the grounds of undue influence unless it can be proved that the transaction is to the manifest disadvantage of the person subject to undue influence.

Undue influence exerted directly by a bank is rare. More usually, the principal debtor exerts it and is deemed to be acting as the bank's agent in the transaction.

The doctrine of undue influence is founded in equity and its basis was stated in *Allcard* v *Skinner* [1887].

Guarantee by a wife or elderly relative

Problems are most likely to occur where a wife guarantees her husband's borrowing or an elderly parent that of their child. Although no undue influence is presumed to exist in such relationships, it can be proved on the facts, e.g. where the wife has neither an interest in, nor gains a benefit from, the transaction: *National Westminster Bank plc* v *Morgan* [1985]. However, provided the bank does not have actual or constructive notice that undue influence has been exerted, the guarantee will not be set aside: *Midland Bank plc* v *Perry* [1988]. In the majority of cases undue influence arises where, at the time of the transaction, a particular relationship of confidence existed between the parties, thus giving rise to a presumption of undue influence: *Tate* v *Williamson* [1866].

A wife or elderly parent must obtain independent legal advice – specifically, the main clauses of the guarantee must be explained.

Principal debtor obtaining the guarantee

It is not advisable to ask the principal debtor to obtain the guarantor's signature. Apart from the obvious risk of forged signature(s), the debtor would almost certainly be deemed to act as the bank's agent and the bank would be responsible for any misrepresentation or undue influence which might be exerted: *Avon Finance Co. Ltd* v *Bridger* [1985]; *Kingsnorth Trust Ltd* v *Bell* [1986]; *Coldunell Ltd* v *Gallon* [1986]; *Bank of Baroda* v *Shah* [1988]; *Midland Bank plc* v *Perry* [1988]; *Midland Bank plc* v *Shephard* [1988]; *Lloyds Bank plc* v *Egremont* [1990].

Guarantee by a customer

The possibility of direct undue influence by a bank arises here. In *Lloyds Bank Ltd* v *Bundy* [1975], for example, the guarantor relied on the bank for financial advice, and the bank failed to avoid the conflict of interest that arose where it took security from its customer to secure the borrowing of another customer, Bundy's son.

The likelihood of the principal debtor being deemed to be the bank's agent is possibly increased where both the principal debtor and guarantor are customers of the bank.

A bank may breach its contractual duty to its customer by failing to explain the guarantee and/or insisting that independent legal advice is received, particularly where:

(a) the guarantor may be under the principal debtor's dominance;
(b) the guarantor is not a business person or otherwise does not fully appreciate such transactions;
(c) most of the guarantor's assets are already charged as security.

Where such a breach of duty occurs, the guarantee will not be set aside for undue influence but the bank may be liable to pay compensation to its customers for any loss incurred as a result of the transaction, e.g. the value of any security sold: *Midland Bank plc* v *Perry* [1988].

Guarantees given by women
Because of experiences of certain cases in the past, lenders take a cautious approach when handling a guarantee given by a woman, especially when she guarantees her husband's liabilities: *Barclays Bank plc* v *O'Brien* [1993]. A woman may claim undue influence and this will invalidate her guarantee. If she is a company director or has her own business interests, it is unlikely for her to succeed in such a claim.

Leading cases relevant in respect of claims of undue influence by a wife are: *Bank of Montreal* v *Stuart* [1911]; *Mackenzie* v *Royal Bank of Canada* [1934]; *Chetwynd-Talbot* v *Midland Bank Ltd* [1982].

3.3.2 Misrepresentation, misapprehension, disclosure of information and mistake

Misrepresentation
The terms of the guarantee must not be misrepresented to the customer. At law, misrepresentation entitles the party misled to avoid the contract, whether the misrepresentation was innocent, negligent or fraudulent.

Misapprehension
An apparent misapprehension about the guarantee must be clarified by the bank, as failure to do so may amount to a breach of its contractual duty (if the guarantor is a customer) or misrepresentation: *Lloyds Bank plc* v *Waterhouse* [1991]; *Royal Bank of Scotland* v *Greenshields* [1914]. Insistence on independent legal advice should avoid such problems: *Barclays Bank plc* v *O'Brien* [1993]; *Davies* v *London & Provincial Marine Insurance Co.* [1878]. A bank is *not*

under a duty to explain the terms of a guarantee to a guarantor who is not a customer of the bank: *O'Hara* v *Allied Irish Banks Ltd* [1985].

Disclosure

A bank owes no duty to volunteer information about its customer which might influence a prospective guarantor: *Cooper* v *National Provincial Bank Ltd* [1945]; *National Provincial Bank of England Ltd* v *Glanusk* [1913]. The guarantors must make their own enquiries about the principal debtor. A duty does exist, however, to correct any obvious mistaken belief the guarantor holds about the principal debtor. This poses a problem, because correcting the belief would almost certainly be a breach of the duty of confidentiality. The correct course of action is therefore to obtain the customer's consent before making the disclosure, or arrange a meeting where questions can be put to the principal debtor directly by the guarantor. If the principal debtor fails to co-operate, the guarantee can be declined.

Mistake

Guarantors may subsequently claim that they mistook the nature of the document signed: *Saunders* v *Anglia Building Society* [1971]. However, to avoid a guarantee on this ground, the guarantors must show that they acted without negligence. Thus, provided the guarantors understand the nature of the guarantee, signing the guarantee without reading it will not warrant it being set aside: *Howatson* v *Webb* [1907].

3.3.3 Value and enforceability of the guarantee

The following points should be kept in mind.

Legal capacity

The guarantor must be legally able to enter into the transaction, e.g. they must be an adult and not an undischarged bankrupt. A bankruptcy search at the Land Charges Registry can be made in this latter respect using form K16. This will reveal any petitions or bankruptcy inhibitions against the guarantor. Added protection is provided by the standard 'indemnity clause' which ensures that the guarantee is directly enforceable against the guarantor even if the borrowing is not. Under the Minors' Contracts Act 1987, a guarantee of a loan to a minor is enforceable even though the loan itself is not.

Guarantor's means

The guarantor should have adequate personal means to honour the guarantee when called upon to do so. It is preferable to obtain a joint and several guarantee, as this puts the bank in a stronger position against each of the guarantors if it has to enforce the guarantee (see 3.8.5). This is standard banking practice.

Obtain a status enquiry for the full amount of the guarantee if the prospective guarantor is not a customer of the bank. Make it clear on the form whether it is an individual guarantee or a joint and several co-guarantee. In the case of co-guarantors, a status enquiry for the full amount should be made against each co-guarantor.

If any reply is unsatisfactory, decline the guarantee or ask for supporting security.

Security
There must be a sufficient margin in the value of security taken in support of the guarantee.

Consumer Credit Act 1974
If the lending is regulated by the Consumer Credit Act 1974, the guarantee must be executed in accordance with the requirement of the Act.

3.3.4   Accuracy of details

Ensure that:

(a)   the name of the borrower is correctly spelt;
(b)   the guarantee is dated;
(c)   an address for service of demand for payment is inserted;
(d)   all other insertions are initialled by all the parties to the guarantee (it is good practice to have each page initialled by all parties);
(e)   in respect of a guarantee for a limited amount, insert the limit in words and figures.

3.3.5   Supported guarantee

Ensure that the correct form of charge is taken.

3.4   TAKING THE SECURITY

3.4.1 Guarantee sent to the guarantor's solicitor or bank for execution

Solicitor's details
Obtain the name and address of the solicitor. If necessary conduct a status enquiry.

Explanation of the guarantee

Explain the principal clauses of the guarantee to the guarantor to avoid the guarantor being under any misapprehension. Take care not to misrepresent the contents. Misrepresentation may arise where the bank voluntarily asumes the role of giving advice: *Redmond* v *Allied Irish Banks plc* [1987]. It is good practice to make a file note of the interview noting that the principal clauses were explained and facts clarified. This is particularly important where an awareness/freewill clause is to be signed confirming that the guarantor was advised to take independent legal advice but the offer was declined and the bank was prepared to accept this.

The bank has a duty to explain the nature and effect of security documents which it is taking from the customer or third party: *Cornish* v *Midland Bank plc* [1985]. If a person giving a guarantee is a customer also, it is a bank's duty of good faith to advise the customer: *Barclays Bank plc* v *Khaira* [1992].

Guarantee form

Ensure that the names of the principal debtor and guarantor are correctly spelt. Mark in pencil who is to sign the independent legal advice or freewill clause. Complete one form for each guarantor if there are co-guarantors.

Instructions for execution

Send the forms direct to the bank or solicitor. Do not release the guarantee to the principal debtor or to the guarantor to obtain the latter's signature.

The bank or solicitor should be instructed to:

(a)   Attest the guarantor's signature and sign an attestation clause to the effect that they have explained the terms of the guarantee to the guarantor.

(b)   Obtain the guarantor's signature to the freewill clause, where the guarantor does not wish to obtain independent legal advice before executing the guarantee. (The clause states that the guarantor was given the opportunity to obtain legal advice before executing the guarantee, but chose not to do so, having fully understood the nature of the liability incurred under it.)

(c)   Add a confirmation to the attestation clause that where the guarantor signed in a language other than English, the terms of the guarantee were explained in that other language and that the guarantor signed having fully understood the nature of the guarantee. The name, address and occupation of the witness should be inserted so that it is possible to trace the witness if it becomes necessary.

31

(d)   Date the guarantee with the date of execution.

(e)   Give a copy of the executed guarantee to each guarantor. In the case of Consumer Credit Act guarantees, the copy need not be given at the time of execution but must be sent within seven days of its execution. The surety is entitled to a copy of not only a guarantee but also of the regulated agreement and a copy of a statement later on (if he requests): s.107 Consumer Credit Act.

(f)   Post the executed guarantee direct to the bank.

After receipt
After the guarantee is returned, check that it is signed by *all* the guarantors, dated, that all insertions are initialled, and that it is properly witnessed and attested.

3.4.2   Co-guarantors

A co-guarantee must be signed by all co-guarantors to be valid: *National Provincial Bank Ltd* v *Brackenbury* [1906]. Similarly, a forgery of one of the signatures renders the guarantee void: *James Graham & Co. (Timber) Ltd* v *Southgate Sands* [1985].

3.4.3   Guarantees by partners

A partner has no implied authority to give a guarantee in the firm's name. Thus, express written authority from all partners is required. In respect of partnership borrowing, ensure that the guarantee is conducive to the operation of the business. Do not take a guarantee from a partner for the firm's account as he is liable in any event.

3.4.4   Guarantees by limited companies

Carry out a company search and a mortgage register search to ensure that the company still exists and that there are no adverse charges or entries which would affect the guarantee.

Despite the abolition of the *ultra vires* rule by the Companies Act 1989, it is prudent to check:

(a)   the company's memorandum of association to ensure that the company has the power to give guarantees – if it does not, the objects clause should be altered by special resolution in a general meeting and certified copy of the resolution obtained;

(b)   the articles of association to ensure that the directors have the power to give guarantees on behalf of the company.

Also ensure that giving the guarantee is to the commercial benefit of the company: *Charterbridge Corporation Ltd v Lloyds Bank Ltd* [1969]. (Again, it is probably prudent not to rely on the abolition of the *ultra vires* rule.) Extra care must be taken in this respect where an inter-company guarantee is proposed. Please note that different banks adopt different practices in relation to company objects clauses.

In *Ford and Carter Ltd* v *Midland Bank Ltd* [1979], the problems of a short cut, in respect of mutual guarantees entered into by the companies when a bank lends to a group, were highlighted.

If directors have a personal interest in the guarantee (*Victors Ltd* v *Lingard* [1927]), e.g. the loan guaranteed is to be used to repay loans to the company from directors, the resolution authorising the guarantee should be passed by a quorum of independent directors.

A guarantee given by a foreign company must not infringe the laws of the country concerned. To avoid the guarantee being challenged by the creditors of the company on its insolvency, a certificate of solvency must be obtained from the directors. In such cases ensure that all resolutions and documents relating to the guarantee comply with the legal requirements.

3.4.5   Consumer Credit Act guarantees

Follow these steps:

1.   Give the surety the opportunity to obtain legal advice.
2.   Explain the terms and clauses of the guarantee to the guarantor.
3.   Have the guarantee signed on the bank's premises.
4.   Give a copy of the guarantee to the guarantor after it is signed.
5.   In respect of a loan, give a copy of the loan agreement, if already signed by the principal debtor, to the guarantor. If it has not been signed, send a copy (signed on the bank's premises) to the guarantor within seven days.
6.   In respect of an overdraft, give a copy of the facility letter to the guarantor at the time the guarantee is signed, or within seven days of the principal debtor signing the facility letter.
7.   Copies of security documents referred to in the facility letter must be given to the guarantor within seven days of signing the guarantee.

3.5 MONITORING THE SECURITY

3.5.1 Status enquiry

If a status enquiry on the guarantor was made, keep a copy with the guarantee. Make a diary note to renew the status enquiry at six monthly or yearly intervals to ensure the financial stability of the guarantor. A fresh status enquiry should be obtained if a new guarantee for a higher amount is sought. Under their versions of the 'Code of Practice', not all banks will reply to status enquiries without their customers' consent or specific instructions.

It is also good practice to remind the guarantor of his or her liability under the guarantee five years after the guarantee is executed. Some banks also remind the guarantor of his or her continuing obligations in cases where an interval occurs between one facility being repaid and another one being arranged.

3.5.2 Increased facility

If the principal requests an increased facility, it is better to obtain a new guarantee for the whole of the increased facility than to take a new guarantee for the additional facility. Where an unlimited guarantee was taken, the usual 'all monies' clause renders this legally unnecessary.

When the new guarantee is executed, the original guarantee can be placed with the cancelled papers, but do *not* mark it 'cancelled' just in case the bank needs to rely on it in the future (*see* page 39).

3.5.3 Deterioration in debtor's position or unacceptable conduct

If the bank is aware that the debtor's position is deteriorating, e.g.where the overdraft facility is funding gambling, a bank may consider it owes an ethical (not legal) duty to protect the guarantor. A tripartite meeting can be arranged between the guarantor, debtor and the bank, where the situation can be discussed without the risk of breaching the duty of confidentiality.

If the debtor continues such conduct, make a demand for repayment on the debtor. This fixes the guarantor's liability. Alternatively, the guarantor may choose to give notice of determination.

3.6 STANDARD CLAUSES IN A BANK GUARANTEE

1. Continuation of the account This clause protects a bank if, after determination of the guarantee, it fails to break the guarantor's account and open a new account to prevent the rule in *Clayton's* case [1816] operating to its detriment.

Put simply, it preserves the guarantee when the account swings into credit through payments in the ordinary course of business. Such a clause was held to be effective in *Westminster Bank Ltd* v *Cond* [1940].

2. *Consideration* Bank guarantees always include a statement of the consideration given by the bank, although this is not strictly necessary: *United Dominions Trust Ltd* v *Beech* [1972]. A guarantee by deed does not require any consideration.

The consideration is not stated to be a fixed amount, because the guarantee would then be ineffective if the bank does not lend the stated, fixed amount: *Burton* v *Gray* [1873]. Unless the guarantor has an authority to give consideration, it will not be considered as valid: *Deutsche Bank AG* v *Ibrahim and others* [1992].

A guarantee of a non-operative account poses a problem, because if no further funds are lent and the account is not operated normally, the bank cannot prove that it allowed, say, the debtor time to pay or provided continuing facilities. Technically the consideration would be 'past' and therefore, at law, no consideration.

In such cases the bank should either:

(a) refuse the guarantee; or
(b) make a demand on the debtor to repay (in response, the proposed guarantor can request the bank to give time to the debtor against the security of the guarantee); or
(c) have the guarantee executed as a deed.

3. *Repayable on demand* By this clause the guarantors undertake that, on a written demand being made to them, they will discharge all monies and liabilities owing by the principal debtor to the bank.

The effect is that the six-year limitation period (Limitation Act 1980) in which the guarantee can be enforced does not begin to run until a formal demand for repayment is made. In respect of a guarantee by deed, the limitation period is 12 years.

4. *Continuing security* This clause ensures that the guarantee covers the outstanding balance at any time and not the specific sum advanced. It thereby avoids the operation of the rule in *Clayton's* case [1816] to the bank's detriment. Without this clause, every payment in would reduce the amount secured by the guarantee, while every payment out would constitute a new debt that would not be covered by the guarantee. If supporting security is held, this clause offers no protection against a subsequent mortgagee who gives notice to the bank: *Deeley* v *Lloyds Bank Ltd* [1912].

5. All monies/whole debt This makes the guarantor liable for the total amount owing, including all interest and costs, irrespective of the amount demanded. It is usual, however, for this clause to include a limit on the guarantor's actual liability to pay.

This clause is included because:

(a) It prevents the guarantors claiming a contribution from any co-guarantors where the guarantors have paid only part of the debt, even though this is their proportionate share and/or the actual limit specified in the guarantee.

(b) The guarantor loses the right to prove in the debtor's insolvency in competition with the bank: *Re Sass* [1896].

(c) It prevents the the guarantor suing the principal debtor for the amount paid to the bank under the guarantee.

(d) The guarantor is unable to exercise the right of subrogation against a proportionate share of any securities deposited in support of the guarantee by the principal debtor or a third party. ('Subrogation' is to gain another party's rights.)

6. Indemnity This ensures that if the sums due cannot be recovered from the principal debtor because of their contractual incapacity or other legal limitation, the bank can recover the monies advanced directly from the guarantor as principal debtor, i.e. the guarantor incurs primary liability in such a case. This clause is useful when lending to a club, society or church. (Guarantees of loans to minors are enforceable by virtue of s. 2, Minors' Contracts Act 1987, even though the loan to the minor is not enforceable.)

7. Variation of terms This clause gives the bank power, without further consent from the guarantor and without affecting the guarantors' liability under the guarantee:

(a) to vary arrangements with any party to the guarantee;
(b) release securities to the debtor: or
(c) enter into a voluntary arrangement with the debtor in the event of their insolvency.

The bank is thereby given flexibility in its dealings with the guarantor, whereas at common law any alteration of the terms of the contract or release of securities without the guarantor's consent would discharge the guarantee.

8. Power to open a new account with the debtor notwithstanding the determination of the guarantee Although the validity of a clause allowing the bank to continue the debtor's account after notice of determination by the guarantor was recognised in *Westminster Bank Ltd* v *Cond* [1940], the usual practice is to break the account and open a new account for all future transactions.

9. Sufficient demand A demand in writing has to be made to the debtor before action can be taken to enforce the guarantee. Problems can be encountered in proving to the court that the demand was made before action to enforce the guarantee was taken, where the guarantor does not acknowledge receipt of the bank's letters.

The clause overcomes this problem providing that the demand and the method by which it is served comply with the clause.

10. Determination The guarantee may include a clause which makes the guarantor liable for any advance made within the limits of the guarantee during the period of notice for determination prescribed by the guarantee.

If the clause is omitted, the guarantor could repay the outstanding liability and have the guarantee cancelled, thereby not incurring liability for further advances made to the principal debtor during the period of notice: *Coulthart* v *Clementson* [1879].

By a clause in the bank guarantee forms, a guarantor agrees in advance to variation so that the guarantee shall not be discharged if:

(a) extra time after the due date for payment is given to the borrower, or the borrower obtains the release of securities lodged with the bank or enters into an arrangement with the bank to vary the terms of the advance or compound the debt; and

(b) the co-guarantor's liabilities are released or security he has given is discharged.

Although this type of clause is valid it must be appropriately worded: *National Bank of Nigeria Ltd* v *Oba M.S. Awolesi* [1964].

11. Security from the principal debtor This clause prevents the guarantor from competing with the bank in the principal debtor's insolvency, by proving for sums paid under the guarantee in the insolvency, by taking security from them, or by suing them: *Re Sass* [1896].

12. Additional guarantees　The guarantee is stated to be in addition to, and not in substitution for, any other guarantees for the borrowing. It protects the bank should the guarantor argue that a subsequent guarantee was given in substitution for the original.

Where an additional guarantee is required, the original guarantee should be cancelled and a fresh guarantee obtained for the full amount.

13. Conclusive evidence　This clause is included to avoid the guarantor disputing the extent of the principal debtor's liability.

Under it the guarantor agrees to accept a written statement from the bank of the amount owing to the bank by the principal debtor as conclusive evidence of the debt: *Bache & Co. (London) Ltd* v *Banque Vernes et Commerciale de Paris SA* [1973].

14. Change in the constitution of the parties　This clause avoids any problem caused by the principal debtor (or the bank) changing its name, constitution or amalgamating with another person; or through the insolvency, death or dissolution of the principal debtor.

Inclusion of the clause makes it unnecessary for the the bank to break the debtor's account to preserve the guarantor's liability. In the case of partnership, the account must be broken to preserve the liability of a former partner.

15. Notice of death　This clause prevents the guarantee being determined by receipt of notice of the guarantor's death and the personal representatives remain liable.

Without the inclusion of this clause, the bank would have to stop the debtor's account upon receiving notice, in order to prevent the rule in *Clayton's* case [1816] operating to its detriment. Despite the inclusion of the clause, normal practice on receiving notice of death is to inform the guarantor's personal representatives of their continuing liability under the guarantee, provide a copy of the guarantee if requested to do so, and specify the notice necessary to determine their liability.

If the guarantor's estate is insufficient to cover the liability, or the bank does not wish to increase the liability, determine the guarantee by giving notice to the principal debtor.

16. Choice of law　Under this clause the guarantor agrees that the guarantee of the principal debtor's UK debts is made under English law, but that the guarantor will submit to alternative jurisdiction if the bank so requires. A receiver or manager of a company appointed in one part of the United Kingdom may exercise his powers in relation to property situated in any other part of the United Kingdom provided their exercise is not inconsistent with the law applicable there: *Ford and Carter Ltd* v *Midland Bank Ltd* [1979].

17. Action against the principal debtor   By this clause the guarantors agree that they will be liable for the ultimate balance due to the bank from the principal debtor, and that they will not take any legal action against the principal debtor until any balance owing after the guarantee has been honoured, is repaid to the bank: *Davis* v *Humphreys* [1840].

18. Joint and several liability   This applies where there are two or more co-guarantors and it prevents any dispute about the nature of the liability.

It is also advisable to include a clause stating that the release of a joint and several guarantor does not release the other(s) from liability: *Mercantile Bank of Sydney* v *Taylor* [1893]. Where a joint and several guarantee is worded to stipulate that the guarantee will be a continuing security until three months' written notice of determination is given by each of the co-guarantors, written notice by one co-guarantor will not be effective.

19. Insolvency   A clause is included which entitles the bank to hold a guarantee uncancelled for at least 24 months after the borrowing guaranteed has been repaid.

This avoids loss should any payment to the bank made in discharge or reduction of the principal debt be subsequently avoided as a preference, i.e. have to be repaid to the liquidator or trustee. (Twenty-four months is the maximum period in which a preference can be set aside.)

The clause also affords protection where a floating charge is taken from a company in substitution for a guarantee of the company's borrowing and this charge is invalidated by the insolvency of the company within 12 months of giving the charge.

Thus, to preserve the guarantor's liability, it is vital that the guarantee is not released or cancelled until the end of the specified period.

20. Charges and costs   A clause is included providing that any charges and costs incurred by the bank in enforcing the security can be recovered from the guarantor if they cannot be recovered from the principal debtor.

By this clause, the guarantor agrees to be liable as a primary debtor.

This clause protects the bank in cases where the principal debtor is not liable because of incapacity, thus making a guarantee void. In these cases the guarantor has direct liability to indemnify the bank for any loss it may incur.

21. Guarantee to remain the bank's property   Even though the borrowing originally guaranteed is repaid, an 'all monies', 'continuing security' guarantee remains enforceable until it is determined by notice in accordance with its terms.

As guarantors rarely determine their guarantees after the original borrowing is repaid, it is clearly in the bank's interest to retain ownership of the guarantee form because, subject only to the statutory limitation period after a demand is made, it operates as an open-ended security for any future indebtedness of the principal debtor.

22. Currency conversion   Where the guarantee liability is in a foreign currency, this clause gives the bank the right to convert such liability to sterling.

23. Lien   A guarantee that contains this clause gives the bank a (contractual) lien on any securities, property, any account credit balances and items held in safe custody. (This is not a true lien because a lien arises by operation of law, not by agreement as here.)

24. Separate suspense account   This clause enables a bank to open a separate suspense account and pay into it any sums received, recovered or realised under the guarantee, without any obligation to appropriate (apply) those sums in reduction of the sums due or owing by the debtor.

25. Evidence   To facilitate obtaining judgment against the guarantor, a clause can be included which:

(a)   renders admissible as evidence of the amount outstanding any award or judgment obtained by the bank against the debtor: *Bache & Co (London) Ltd* v *Banque Vernes et Commerciale de Paris SA* [1973]; and

(b)   provides that any statement of account supplied by the bank is conclusive evidence against the guarantor of the amount for the time being due to the bank from the debtor.

26. Consumer Credit Act guarantees   If the facility given to the debtor falls within the Consumer Credit Act 1974, a 'Guarantee and indemnity subject to the Consumer Credit Act 1974' form must be executed. This contains most of the standard guarantee clauses.

The form provides for the insertion of the name and addresses of the principal debtor, the guarantor (surety) as indemnifier, the amount, and an address for service of documents. The guarantor must sign the form within the box provided.

27. Realisation of security by bank A clause in the guarantee sometimes provides that (e.g. in cases where the bank holds security from the principal debtor and the guarantor) the bank can realise securities in such manner as it may deem fit. The guarantor then cannot claim that the bank did not act properly in realising the security at the time of selling the property, thereby increasing his liability. A clause may also state that the guarantee obtained is 'in addition to' and not 'in substitution of' any other guarantees held.

Note: Bank guarantee forms are complex legal documents: additions, deletions or amendments must not be made to them without reference to the bank's legal department. Ill-considered changes may result in the guarantee proving to be unenforceable: *Westminster Bank Ltd v Sassoon* [1926].

3.7 REQUESTS FOR INFORMATION BY THE GUARANTOR

3.7.1 Balance enquiries

When a guarantor asks for the outstanding balance under his liability, the following information can be given.

(a) Balance is less than the amount of the guarantee
Here the bank can disclose the actual balance but the guarantor should be reminded that this is the current balance.

(b) Balance is greater than the amount of the guarantee
Inform the guarantor that the guarantee is being fully relied on; do not disclose the actual balance outstanding.

(c) A credit balance exists
Inform the guarantor that the guarantee is currently not being relied on; do not disclose the actual credit balance.

If, on the basis of this information, the guarantor asks the bank to cancel the liability, remind the guarantor of the notice period for determination – usually one to three months – and that he/she would be liable for the outstanding debit balance at the date the notice period expires. If necessary, arrange a meeting with the debtor and guarantor to discuss the account; additional security can be requested.

If the customer confirms that the overdraft facility will not be utilised and that the account will be maintained in credit in future, the bank can cancel the guarantee if it considers that it will not need to rely on it.

If, however, the customer confirms that the guarantee is being relied on, e.g.

to fund future business, ask the guarantor to give written notice to determine the guarantee on the expiry date. Subsequently advise the guarantor of the liability if the borrowing has to be recovered from them.

In this latter case, stop the customer's account and open a new account which must be maintained in credit or appropriately secured.

3.7.2   Action against co-guarantors

Do not disclose information or action taken by the bank against co-guarantors.

3.7.3   Copies of cheques or account statements

Such requests must be refused because of the bank's duty of confidentiality: *Tournier* v *National Provincial & Union Bank of England* [1924]. If possible, however, discover the reason for the enquiry.

3.7.4   Consumer Credit Act guarantees

The Consumer Credit Act 1974, s.107 gives the guarantor of a loan or overdraft regulated by the Act a statutory right (on payment of a small fee) to a statement of the principal debtor's account.

3.8   DETERMINATION OF A GUARANTEE

3.8.1   Demand by the bank

The following actions should be taken:

1. If the debtor's account has been conducted unsatisfactorily, first make a demand for repayment against the debtor. Stop the account to prevent the rule in *Clayton's* case [1816] operating to the bank's detriment.
2. If the debtor does not pay, make a demand against the guarantor.
3. If the guarantee is unlimited, the total amount outstanding at the date of the demand, including all costs and interest, can be demanded.
4. If the guarantee is limited, make a demand up to the amount of the limit of the guarantee or the balance outstanding, whichever is the smaller sum.
5. If the guarantee was a joint and several co-guarantee, demand the full amount from each co-guarantor.
6. The demand must be made in accordance with the terms of the guarantee to the guarantor's last known address.
7. Do not allow any debit transactions on the account(s) secured after a demand has been made.

8. If the guarantor makes a payment which is less than the total outstanding balance, credit the payment to a separate suspense account or securities realised account. Should the debtor prove to be insolvent, this action preserves the bank's right to claim the full amount outstanding in the insolvency.

9. If the guarantor makes full repayment, credit the debtor's account to adjust the debt.

3.8.2 Notice by the guarantor

The guarantor can determine his guarantee by giving notice in writing (usually three months). The following actions should be taken:

1. Acknowledge the notice in writing, draw the guarantor's attention to the notice period stated in the guarantee (one to three months) and advise the guarantor that he or she will be liable for the debt outstanding at the date the notice expires.

2. Arrange a meeting with the borrower and guarantor to discuss how the account will be conducted during the notice period.

3. Continue to rely on the guarantee up to the end of the notice period.

4. Make a diary note of the date of expiry of the notice so that the debtor's account can be stopped.

5. Decide whether further securities from the debtor should be requested or whether demand on the debtor should be made so that the guarantor's liability is fixed before the notice expires.

After the guarantor has given notice to determine the guarantee, the guarantor can ask the principal debtor to pay even if the bank has not made formal demand for repayment: *Thomas* v *Nottingham Incorporated Football Club Ltd* [1972]. This is an example of equitable right of exoneration.

6. If the guarantor makes payments during the notice period, credit them to a separate suspense or securities realised account.

7. In the case of a limited guarantee, a full payment by the guarantor during the notice period should still be placed in a suspense account to preserve the bank's rights against the debtor. (If the guarantor pays the liabilities in full, all securities held by the bank for the account guaranteed (both direct and third party securities) can be transferred to the guarantor. However, if requested to do so, first refer to head office. Do not release the guarantee, but confirm in writing that there is no immediate liability on the account).

8.   If during the notice period, the guarantor informs the bank that he or she is aware that the debtor is increasing the debt, with the guarantor's consent, make a demand on the debtor in order to fix the guarantor's liability. If the debtor fails to respond, make a demand against the guarantor.

At the end of the notice period, stop the account and open a new account if the bank has agreed to continue to lend without the security of the guarantee , although the bank will be protected if it fails to stop the account because of inclusion of a clause in the guarantee: *Westminster Bank Ltd v Cond* [1940].

3.8.3   Notice by one co-guarantor

The guarantee will allow the bank to release one co-guarantor or depositor of security without affecting its rights against the others. Thus, there is no need to break the account.
The following actions should be taken:

1.   Acknowledge the notice and make a diary note of the date of its expiry.

2.   Take a fresh joint and several guarantee from the remaining guarantors for the continuing account if they agree to apportion the debt. Take a fresh independent guarantee from the guarantor who has given notice for the amount for which they are liable. Upon the expiration of the notice, the guarantor giving notice can be held liable for the whole debt unless the other co-guarantors agree to apportion the debt.

3.   If one or more co-guarantors give notice to determine a proportion of the liability, remind the guarantor(s) that the guarantee cannot be released until the whole liability is repaid.

4.   Although the guarantee provides that it remains effective against remaining co-guarantors, it is advisable not to cancel the liability of a co-guarantor making part payment, because at common law cancellation of their liability would discharge the other co-guarantors.

3.8.4   Change in the constitution of a partnership

Unless expressly agreed otherwise, a guarantee from a partnership will be determined on its dissolution, or where partner retires or joins. A new partner will not be bound by the existing guarantee and a new guarantee must be executed. Partners remain personally liable, of course, for existing partnership borrowing. (**Note**: Bank guarantees provide that a change in the constitution of the bank or the debtor will not determine the guarantee.)

3.8.5 Notice of death

Sole guarantor
On the death of a sole guarantor, the deceased's personal representatives remain liable. The bank should either:

- Write to the personal representatives stating the guarantee liability and explaining the determination procedure and the notice period if it wants to continue to rely on the guarantee; *or*
- Stop the debtor's account and call up the guarantee if the guarantor's estate is not substantial or where it wishes to protect the estate from further liability.

If the personal representatives give notice of determination, consider whether to ask for additional security from the debtor or whether to make a demand on the debtor to fix the guarantor's liability.

Co-guarantor with joint and several liability
Bank guarantees invariably impose joint and several liability on co-guarantors. Joint and several liability:

- enables the bank to exercise the right to combine a credit balance on a co-guarantor's individual account with his/her liability under the guarantee; and
- ensures that the co-guarantor's estate is not discharged by the guarantor's death.

Note: Neither would apply if the guarantee imposed only joint liability.

Depending on the terms of the guarantee, it may not be necessary to break the account. It is not necessary to do so where:

- the guarantee contains a clause which states that the bank's rights are not affected if it fails to break the account: *Westminster Bank Ltd* v *Cond* [1940]; or
- the guarantee contains a clause that, unless notice is given by each surety, the guarantee is not determined: *Egbert* v *National Crown Bank* [1918].

If the guarantee does not contain such a clause:

– break the debtor's account and pass all future transactions through a new account in order to preserve the liability of the deceased guarantor's estate;
– contact the deceased guarantor's personal representatives so that the estate is not distributed.

Principal debtor

Unless otherwise agreed, notice of the the principal debtor's death determines the guarantee, because a guarantor does not promise to be liable for the debts incurred by the debtor's personal representatives.

Break the debtor's account and pass all further entries through a new account. This must be kept in credit or appropriately secured.

3.8.6 Notice of the guarantors' mental incapacity

Sole guarantor

Break the account and make demand on the principal debtor.

Co-guarantors

The other co-guarantors remain liable by virtue of the joint and several liability clause. Thus, there is no need to break the account. Do not make further advances.

3.8.7 Release of the debtor

Do not release the debtor from his or her obligation as this will discharge the guarantor's liability: *Perry* v *National Provincial Bank of England Ltd* [1910]. The legal reasoning is a little complex. Merely agreeing not to sue the debtor does not discharge the guarantee as the debt still exists. If, however, the release is in return for 'value' (consideration), e.g. part repayment, this amounts to an 'accord and satisfaction' which discharges the debtor's debt and therefore means that there no longer is a debt to guarantee.

3.8.8 Death, mental incapacity or insolvency of the principal debtor

The following actions should be taken:

1. Stop the debtor's account on receipt of notice of any of the above events and open a new account.
2. Advise the guarantor and make demand on them.
3. Place any credits received from the guarantor to a separate securities realised account.

3.8.9   Bankruptcy of the guarantor

Sole guarantor
The following actions should be taken:

1. Stop the debtor's account and make demand on the debtor.
2. Prove in the guarantor's bankruptcy for the outstanding debt or for the amount of the guarantee, whichever is the smaller.
3. Place all payments received from the debtor's trustee in bankruptcy to a separate account in order to preserve the bank's right of proof against the debtor for the full amount of the outstanding debt.

Joint and several guarantors
The following actions should be taken:
1. Follow the steps above for a sole guarantor.
2. Obtain a new guarantee signed by the remaining solvent guarantors if no proof is made against the bankrupt guarantor.

3.9   REPAYMENT BY THE PRINCIPAL DEBTOR

A guarantee taken to secure specific lending, i.e. one which does not cover future facilities, can be cancelled upon repayment of the debt by the principal debtor.

If the guarantee is to cover regular borrowing and is expressed to be a continuing security for past and future liabilities, it must not be cancelled.

A letter may, however, be sent confirming that monies have been received but retaining the bank's rights under the guarantee (see also 3.10.1).

3.10   RETENTION OF THE GUARANTEE AND SUBSEQUENT POSITION

3.10.1   Retention of the guarantee
Do not hand over the guarantee or write 'cancelled' across it when a guarantor pays the full amount of the outstanding debt. This enables the bank to rely on the guarantee in the future should it have to. For example, if (unusual) payments into the debtor's account are made and the debtor subsequently becomes insolvent, these may be set aside as preferences. Retaining the guarantee enables the bank to claim under the guarantee for any sums which are held to be preferences, and which it therefore has to repay, as well as the outstanding balance.

3.10.2 Subrogation

A guarantor has the right of subrogation and the right to assume the position of the bank against the debtor, where the guarantor pays the total outstanding debt. For example, the guarantor has the right to take over all securities lodged by the debtor with the bank.

If full repayment is made by a number of co-guarantors, each co-guarantor has a right of subrogation. Written authority from all the relevant co-guarantors should be obtained clarifying how the securities are to be transferred.

Obtain the written authority of the guarantor(s) making repayment for the release of security held.

3.10.3 Contribution

A co-guarantor repaying the debt in full has a right of contribution from the other co-guarantors which can be exercised over any security deposited by them.

In such cases, do not release or transfer the security without written authority from all the relevant parties.

3.10.4 Realisation of debtor's securities

Ensure that the true market price is obtained. Failure to do so renders the bank liable to the guarantor to the extent of the guarantor's resulting additional liability: *Standard Chartered Bank* v *Walker and Walker* [1982].

3.10.5 Cancellation

Make a record when the guarantee is paid, discharged or the limit cancelled, and place the guarantee with the cancelled papers. Only mark the guarantee 'cancelled' if it is certain that the bank will not wish to rely on it in the future.

3.11 ENFORCING A GUARANTEE

Once a bank has enforced its security, it does owe a duty both to the mortgagor and to guarantors of the mortgage debt to exercise reasonable care when it sells the property: *Standard Chartered Bank* v *Walker and Walker* [1982]; *China and South Sea Bank Ltd* v *Tan Soon Gin* [1990].

The guarantor who pays off all the liabilities of the borrower is entitled to the right of subrogation. A demand in writing should be made on the principal debtor first to repay his liabilities. If the debtor fails to pay, make demand in writing to the guarantor at the address for service given in the guarantee and at the last known address.

Where a fixed sum guarantee is held as a security comply as follows:

(i)   If the customer's liability (including interest) exceeds the amount of guarantee, make demand for the total amount of the guarantee plus interest.

(ii)   If the customer's liability is less than the amount of the guarantee given as security, make a demand for the outstanding amount owed plus interest, quoting a daily rate of accrual of interest applicable until payment is made.

If the bank has received a notice of determination of the guarantee, acknowledge the notice, advising the guarantor that the bank will calculate his liability at the expiry of the notice period.

If the guarantor pays less than the amount owed by the customer, credit the monies received to a 'securities realised account'. If the amount paid by the borrower and the guarantor exceeds the outstanding debt, pay the surplus to the guarantor.

If the guarantor pays the customer's entire indebtedness, it is advisable to place the payment received to a suspense account, if a likely claim for preference is anticipated.

Where guarantees from two or more guarantors are obtained, make a demand against each guarantor for the total amount of the guarantee.

If the guarantors pay their proportions separately, place the payment in a suspense account to preserve the bank's claim against the borrower and against each guarantor.

3.12   LETTERS OF COMFORT

Letters of comfort are given to a bank by a parent company in respect of a facility to its subsidiary or associated company. While falling short of a guarantee, they are intended to give some comfort to the lenders that the subsidiary or associate will be kept in a reasonably good financial state so that they can perform their obligations to the bank.

Letters of comfort are often a compromise between the lender requiring the security of a guarantee, and the parent company, which is seeking a firm commitment 'in honour' only. The decision in *Kleinwort Benson Ltd* v *Malaysia Mining Corporation Berhad* [1989] has attempted to clarify whether comfort letters are considered as a legally binding agreement. Whether they are binding or not will depend on the wordings of the comfort letter.

The Court of Appeal decided:

(a)   A comfort letter will be presumed to be legally binding if its wordings include a contractual promise or warranty (i.e. a confirmation as to the present and future), although the absence of promise or warranty as to the future does not rule out the possibility of the comfort letter being binding.

(b)   A comfort letter may be binding in part but not in whole.

If a bank wants to rely on a letter of comfort as legally binding, it must make sure that the wordings include a promise or warranty for the future conduct of the party giving it. A clear intention to bind would constitute a legally binding promise: *Chemco Leasing S.p.A.* v *Rediffusion Ltd* [1987].

For cross-guarantees and intercompany guarantees, see Chapter 6 on Limited companies.

4 Life policies

In addition to the standard clauses contained in most charge forms, the following additional clauses will be found in the legal assignment of life policies:

(a)   The assignor undertakes to pay all the premiums when they fall due and produce premium receipts to the bank. If he fails to do so, the bank may pay them and debit his account.

(b)   A bank has, without the assignor's consent, the right to sell and surrender the policy to the company or any other person, if he fails to meet a demand to pay. This power of sale will be free from the restrictions imposed upon the mortgagee's powers by s. 103 of Law of Property Act 1925.

(c)   The customer agrees that when all the monies owing to the bank have been repaid, the bank will reassign the policy to him at his expense.

Before accepting the policy as security, ascertain the benefits and acceptability of each type of policy.

4.1   TYPES OF POLICY

4.1.1   Term assurance

This policy is for a specified term and the monies are only paid if the assured dies within the term specified in the policy. This policy does not acquire surrender or investment value.

4.1.2   Level term assurance

These policies are only beneficial when used to support 'pension based' mortgages. The sum assured and premium remains fixed over the period.

4.1.3   Decreasing term assurance

This type of policy is mostly used as a 'mortgage protection' policy. The sum assured gradually reduces over the period until no value is left in the policy.

4.1.4   Whole life assurance

These policies provide for payment upon the death of the assured, provided the policy is still in force at the time of his death, and will therefore benefit the named beneficiaries. They may be taken out with or without profits, and acquire an investment value and surrender values. For short term lending they are not attractive as security.

4.1.5   Endowment assurance

Full endowment policy
Most lenders accept these policies as security. This assurance policy provides for payment upon the death of the assured. If the assured is still living after the specified period the policy has an investment and surrender value. It provides for payment of a principal sum with or without profits at a fixed future date, or upon the assured's death, whichever occurs first. Endowment policies taken out with profits will acquire a higher value at maturity, but higher premiums have to be paid for this type of policy. A full endowment policy is mostly accepted as security by the lenders especially where borrowers wish to link their mortgages. Borrowers use an endowment mortgage for the purchase of a domestic property and take out an endowment life policy for a specified period of the mortgage advance. The policy is taken out for the full amount of the loan. The borrower only pays interest on the amount borrowed, and although higher premiums for 'with profits' policies are paid, at the end of the term or if the borrower dies before maturity, good value for money is available. Lenders ask the borrowers to charge the property and life policy as security.

Low cost endowment policy
This is also very common, as premiums are lower with this type of policy. The endowment policy is for a much smaller sum and is linked to a decreasing term assurance. The maturity value of agreed death benefit is maintained at least up to the amount of the loan.

If the borrower dies before the policy matures, then the aggregate sum of the endowment policy plus profits and the decreasing term assurance, will be paid to the lender. This sum will be at least up to the amount of the loan.

If the borrower survives the maturity period, the decreasing term assurance will not have any value, although the endowment policy should increase in value up to the amount of the loan and usually also have some surplus.

4.1.6   Industrial policies

These are 'with profits endowment' policies. They have low surrender values and usually are subject to very low premiums which are paid weekly. They originated in UK factories and industries. There are problems with monitoring frequent premium payments. Premiums are usually required to be paid directly to the assurance company agent and are acknowledged by recording the payment in a premium receipt book.

These policies are not attractive as security.

4.1.7 Settlement/Trust issued under s. 11 Married Women's Property Act 1882

These policies are taken out by a husband on his own life for the benefit of his spouse and/or the children, or a wife on her life for the benefit of her spouse and/or the children.

When the assured dies, the sums due under the policy are held in trust for beneficiaries specified in the policy. They do not form part of the deceased's estate upon death and may not be utilised for the payment of debts.

4.1.8 Family protection policies

This type of policy can provide for:

(a) payment of a capital sum, usually on a sliding scale downwards;

(b) a fixed sum payable, say, quarterly until the expiry of the policy or the purchase of an annuity in favour of the surviving spouse or children. Annual instalments are paid, for example, from the date of death until the deceased would have been 60. The policy may specify a lump sum payment at a certain date.

4.1.9 Paid up policies

If the policy holder is not able to maintain his regular premium payments, the policy may be converted into the paid up policy, so that no further premium payments are required to be paid.

The assurance company in these circumstances will issue a substitute policy with a capital value much smaller than the original value, although the same surrender value will be maintained.

4.1.10 Retirement annuity policies

These policies are usually pension policies. They are not acceptable as security because they can neither be surrendered nor assigned. Lenders, however, may accept deposit of the pension policy without taking a formal charge when providing a 'pension mortgage'.

4.1.11 Accident policies

Accident policies do not acquire surrender values. They are not life policies and are usually not accepted as security. However, some lenders may, as security, accept a legal assignment of the policy if it does not restrict assignment. The lender will receive sums due under the claim if notice is given to the insurers.

4.2 INITIAL SECURITY CONSIDERATIONS

4.2.1 Examination of the policy

Before taking the security ensure that the assignor is financially able to meet the premiums.

1. Ensure that the original policy (not the one marked 'duplicate') is lodged. The duplicate policy can be deemed to be constructive notice of a prior assignment: *Spencer* v *Clarke* [1878]. The bank's charge cannot rank in priority to the earlier charge: *Dearle* v *Hall* [1828].

2. The Policies of Assurance Act 1867 mentions that priority of assignment is determined by the date on which notice is received by the insurance company. Nevertheless, in *Newman* v *Newman* [1885], it was held that when an assignee was on notice of previous assignment, although the assurance company had not been advised, the subsequent assignee could not obtain priority over the prior assignment by giving notice of his charge before that of the other assignee.

3. Check that the beneficiary, who will be signing the charge form, is the person receiving the monies upon death of the life assured and is also the owner of the policy.

If the beneficiary is not the principal debtor, then it will be a third party security, in which case, ensure that the parties are independently advised and standard clauses have been explained to them by the bank to avoid a claim of undue influence.

4. If the policy charged is issued under s. 11(2) of the Married Women's Property Act 1882, the beneficiaries could be described as 'my wife and children'. In *Re Browne's policy* [1903] it was held that this created a trust in favour of the named beneficiaries alive at the time of the claim. The policy could specifically name the beneficiaries, e.g. 'my wife Ann and my children Mark and John'. For these policies, the charge form of legal assignment must be signed by both the proposer and all beneficiaries.

Only accept a Married Women's Property Act policy as security if the beneficiary under the trust is mentioned and is not a minor.

If the beneficiary is not specifically named, do not accept the policy as a security until the insurance company has added the name.

Amend the form of assignment for this purpose. The wordings as advised by the head office should be inserted, and initialled by all the parties signing the assignment.

5. Check that all the material facts are disclosed and the terms of the policy appear to be in accordance with the bank's knowledge of the assignor's situation.

6. Check that the age has been 'admitted'. If not, ask the assignor to lodge the original or a certified copy of his birth certificate with the insurance company. It will then issue an endorsement to be attached to the policy. If the insurance company asks for the actual policy for endorsement, send it and diarise its return.

7. Do not accept policies issued in favour of minors. For policies issued under the Married Women's Property Act 1882 check that other spouse or children are not the beneficiaries.

8. Ensure that there are no unusual conditions, e.g. suicide clause as some insurance policies are not payable in the event of suicide committed within a certain period after its commencement. Check that monies under the policy will be payable in case suicide is committed.

9. Check that there are no other special conditions or restrictions applicable which would affect or reduce the value of the policy, e.g. death due to participation in motor sports or travel by aircraft; restrictions as to residence or occupation; or where death has occurred because of an intentional criminal act: *Amicable Society* v *Bolland* [1830].

10. Ensure that the policy is issued by a reputable insurance company (preferably in the UK) and the premium assured is payable. In respect of policies issued by foreign companies, ensure that premiums are payable in the UK.

11. If consent from the insurance company is required, prior to the signing of the assignment form, this should be obtained.

12. Check that there are no existing charges which will rank ahead of the bank's priority and ascertain from the assurance company if the premiums are paid up-to-date. If not, obtain a current premium receipt, and details of the maturity date (if an endowment policy).

13. Check that the policy is properly stamped, current premiums are paid, and whether the policy has become paid up.

14. Obtain the current surrender value by writing to the company, to ascertain if the policy will be worth accepting as security. Enquire if notice of assignment is received. Surrender value will not be applicable in case of mortgage protection policies or where held as death cover.

If it is an industrial policy, ask for 'cash surrender value'.

For a unit linked policy, more than one type of surrender value may be obtained.

15. The cooling off period of 10 days when a new term life policy is offered as a security is allowed. It may be subject to cancellation within that period.

16. When enquiring the surrender value, if the company advises of prior assignments, obtain the charge, and ensure that reassigned discharged documents are retained as security with the policy, as they form a chain of title. The assurance company will require these to be produced when the policy is surrendered, matures or is paid on the death of the life assured.

17. Check that the assignor has an assignable interest, i.e. there are no restrictions in the policy preventing the assignment, and that the proposer has an insurable interest: *Dalby* v *India and London Life Assurance Co.* [1854]. A life policy may be assigned by someone who has no insurable interest in the life insured: *Ashley* v *Ashley* [1892].

18. Check the policy benefits: i.e. a specified sum, or a sum linked to units in a unit trust fund, with or without profits, and when the sum is payable.

19. To ascertain the strength of security and the margin required, security should be valued. The value will depend on the following:

(a) *Capital value*, which is the minimum amount the company will pay with bonuses upon the beneficiary's death (or in the case of an endowment policy to the assured on survival to a fixed future date upon maturity).

(b) *Amount of bonus*, payable on a with profits endowment policy, or with profits whole life policy, or death of the policy holder.

(c) *Surrender value*, which the policy will acquire.

(d) *Stability value*, i.e. surrender value which increases as future premiums are paid.

A 'without profits' policy will be a fixed sum policy.

A 'with profits' policy would include bonuses, but higher premium payments will have to be paid.

Index linked policies will provide protection of their real value against inflation.

20. Take care if a children's deferred policy is lodged as security (a parent takes out a policy on the life of the child and in his favour), as usually these policies are valueless. They create a trust in favour of a minor, who cannot execute the assignment.

A parent is not likely to have a financial interest in the survival of a minor or an insurable interest in the life of his child. But a parent may insure the life of a successful, earning child for his benefit.

A parent can also insure his child's life and fix a maturity date when he attains a specified age when the sums due under the insurance will be paid to the child. The policy will then be the parent's property until the specified age is reached: *Re Engelbach's Estate* [1923]. Check that the age has been admitted on the policy.

21.   Industrial policies are not attractive because of the difficulty of realisation and monitoring. Normally no surrender value is required. It will be necessary to check with the head office before accepting them as security.

22.   Pension plan policies should not be accepted as security, as they cannot be satisfactorily assigned.

23.   A separate charge form for each policy assigned must be taken.

Because insurance is a contract of the utmost good faith – *uberrimae fidei* – if the proposer does not disclose material facts the contract is void. Material facts mean the facts that would influence a prudent insurer to decide if he should insure the risk (i.e. risk of fraud) or quote the premium rate: *Woolcott* v *Sun Alliance and London Insurance Ltd* [1978].

4.3   TAKING THE SECURITY OF A FIRST LEGAL ASSIGNMENT

A life policy is transferable by assignment, but the assignee will not have a better legal right than the assignor.

4.3.1   Initial considerations

1.   Obtain the original policy.

2.   Inspect the details, e.g. identify the parties who will be signing the document, the proposer, and the beneficiary. Examine the clauses for any restrictions/consents, insurable interests, *uberrimae fidei* age is admitted, suicide clause, cooling off period, the non-payment of premiums. Check that the premiums are payable in sterling in the UK and issued by a reputable company in the UK. Ensure that it is not a trust, and is assignable. Ascertain the amount payable, the term and the benefits.

3.   Establish the surrender value to ensure that it is sufficient for the purposes of the bank. Also enquire if notice of any prior assignments and re-assignments is received. If so, obtain them and retain with the deeds to prove a good chain of title.

4.   Check that premiums are paid up-to-date by obtaining a current premium receipt or enquire from the insurance company. Obtain previous discharged documents forming a chain of title to the policy.

5.   For an industrial policy, ask for sight of the premium receipt book and make a record in the diary for 12 months.

6.   Make a diary note for any options, and maturity or expiry date at least two months before the applicable date.

4.3.2   Before taking the assignment form

1.   Most banks have two separate assignment forms – one for own borrowing and one for a third party borrowing. Choose the correct form.
2.   A separate assignment form for each policy charged must be used. But for policies issued in a series the same form can be used.
3.   In the case of a new policy, do not have the form executed when the proposal form is signed, but when the policy is issued and first premium paid.
4.   Write to the assurance company for a standing order or direct debit mandate to ensure regular payments. When the mandate is received tell the customer the reason for payment by this method and ask him to sign the mandate.

   If it is not possible to arrange for payment as above, make a record in the diary to check that payments are made regularly, or ask for a current premium receipt to be produced.
5.   All persons having monetary interest or trustee interest (both the proposer and beneficiary) must sign the form.
6.   Where a trust policy is charged, check that the beneficiary is named and is not a minor, and include the trustee as a mortgagor. Additional clauses as required by the head office will be inserted against the initials of the parties to the form. Inspect the document of trust.

4.3.3   Completing the assignment form

An assignment of a life policy must comply with s. 5 of the Policies of Assurance Act 1867, i.e. the assignment must be either by an endorsement on the policy itself or by a separate document of assignment in the form laid down in the Act. It must be signed and witnessed.

1.   Insert full names and addresses of the debtor/assignor/life assured; the amount insured (mark with or without profits, or if it is a reducing sum policy); the date of the policy; policy number; the amount secured (if limited limit to be entered); and applicable interest rate, if own account form is used.
2.   Date the form on the day of execution. All insertions and deletions must be initialled by all parties to the form.

   According to the Law of Property Act s.136 a legal assignment of a chose in action may only be made by the assignor by a signed written document. Assignment must be made either by endorsement of the policy or by way of a separate assignment.
3.   Explain the standard clauses in the form, and keep an interview file note.

Provide an opportunity to obtain independent legal advice. If not required, the awareness clause must be signed and retained with the form.

If the form is to be sent to another branch, bank or solicitors, the same procedure outlined in Chapter 3 for the execution of the guarantee form should be followed.

4. When the executed form is returned, check that it is executed properly.

5. Make a diary note for a few days before the maturity date on which the policy is payable.

6. Send the direct debit or standing order mandate, signed by the assignor, to the company for future premiums to be directly paid. Make a diary note for payment of monthly premiums on due dates. Also check them yearly.

For industrial policies ask the assignor to bring the premium receipt book to the branch to make a note of date the premiums are paid.

7. On the day the form is executed, give notice of assignment to the company in duplicate. Ask the company to return a copy as an acknowledgement with any applicable fee enclosed. Some companies require notice to be sent to their head office with a copy of the assignment form. Check the clauses for this purpose.

Industrial policies may require the policy to be sent to the company for endorsement.

Giving notice is important because:

(a) Priority of equal charges is established by the date of receipt of notice by the insurance company: *Dearle* v *Hall* [1828]. Under the Policies of Assurance Act it is necessary to complete the assignment by giving notice.

(b) The bank can sue on the policy in its own name.

(c) On acknowledgement of receipt, the insurance company is committed to pay policy monies only to the bank.

(d) It sets the limit at which the insurance company can exercise set off of any claims which it may have against the policy holder.

Giving notice will not provide these protections to the bank, if it had constructive notice of an existing assignment: *Spencer* v *Clarke* [1878].

8. Make a diary note for acknowledgement (10 to 15 days).

9. When acknowledgement is received, check that it is signed, stamped by the company, dated, and that all enquiries are answered. Hold the acknowledgement with the policy, prior assignments and reassignments, last

current premium receipt, and the assignment form.

10.   If the acknowledgement indicates a prior notice of assignment or that the company itself has a charge over the policy:

(a)   retain the form of assignment and reassignment;

(b)   check that the date of the bank's assignment is after that of the prior reassignment, otherwise a new charge will be required;

(c)   write for confirmation of reassignment from the other bank if prior assignment or reassignment is lost.

4.4   TAKING EQUITABLE ASSIGNMENT

Banks seldom take an equitable assignment of a life policy as security.

1.   An equitable assignment can be taken either by lodging the policy informally or lodging it with the memorandum of deposit. If the customer deposits the policy with intent, but without the memorandum of deposit:

(a)   Make a record of an interview note to avoid a claim that the policy was lodged for safekeeping. This type of security cannot be taken from the third party without the charge form.

(b)   To strengthen the security take a memorandum of deposit, so that the protection of the clauses in the form are available. A memorandum of deposit executed by deed by an irrevocable power of attorney in favour of the assignee will enable the sale to be made without reference to the court.

2.   Obtain the original policy and check all the details as outlined in the legal assignment earlier.

3.   Give the notice of assignment to the insurance company. Provided the bank is not on constructive notice of the charge, the bank, by giving notice, will gain priority over prior assignees, who have taken on assignment but not given notice.

4.   If the bank and other equitable assignees fail to give notice, priority will be determined upon the date of the charge irrespective of whether the equitable charge was in writing or by way of deposit: *Dearle* v *Hall* [1828].

5.   It is important that a satisfactory explanation is given if a duplicate policy and not the original one is lodged as security.

4.5 ASSIGNMENT BY A LIMITED COMPANY

1. A limited company may charge a policy taken out on the life of one of its directors or executives (Keyman policy), and may charge the policy to secure its borrowing in cases where it is a proposer and beneficiary.

2. It follows the same procedure as that of an assignment or charge by an individual, but the following additional points must be borne in mind.

Examine memorandum and articles of association to check:

(a) the purpose of advance is within its objects clause and it is not in breach of Companies Acts;
(b) company's/directors' borrowing powers;
(c) it has power to give security;
(d) personal interests of directors;
(e) if the form is required to be sealed by the company.

3. Obtain a search on the company, its directors, and a copy of the mortgage register.

4. A certified copy of Resolution (borrowing and charging) from the company should be obtained.

Registration at Companies House is not necessary.

4.6 SECOND LEGAL ASSIGNMENT

Banks rarely accept second legal assignment of policy as security. Only when there is some equity in surrender value, they may sometimes accept it as security.

4.6.1 Initial considerations

1. Ensure that the policy is 'with profits' and in force for at least two to three years, otherwise it will not acquire a surrender value.

2. The bank cannot have a legal title to the policy, although it will receive equity, if any, from the proceeds of the policy.

3. The bank will not have power of sale or surrender or receive the monies on maturity without the assignor's co-operation, even if the prior mortgagee is repaid.

4. If the bank serves notice to the insurance company, without the banks' co-operation, the mortgagor cannot receive monies under the policy.

4.6.2 Taking second legal assignment

The procedure is the same as that of the first legal assignment except:

1. Some banks have special forms for this type of charge, others amend their

61

forms by adding a clause, initialled by all the parties to the form.

2.   Apart from checking the policy and completing the details as already mentioned in first legal assignment, the schedule in the charge form must be completed with details of prior assignment.

3.   Ensure, from the prior assignee, the amount secured by their assignment. Obtain the surrender value from the prior assignee to establish the bank's equity, by deducting from the surrender value the amount owing to the prior assignee.

4.   If the first mortgagee and insurance company are not the same, give notice of assignment to all prior assignees so that the surplus monies are remitted to the bank on maturity or surrender of the policy.

5.   If the prior mortgage assignment is repaid, obtain reassignment of the earlier mortgage and take a fresh assignment.

6.   Upon surrender or maturity or repayment of the liability, reassign the assignment. Release the mortgage with the policy and earlier re-assignments to the subsequent assignee, with any surplus monies. Release it to the assignor if there is no subsequent assignee.

4.7   CLAUSES IN THE LIFE POLICY MORTGAGE FORM

A bank's legal mortgage of a life policy includes the following standard clauses:

(a)   All monies clause.

(b)   Continuing security clause.

(c)   Assignment of the benefit of the policy to the bank with an obligation that the bank reassigns the policy to the mortgagor once the loan is repaid and to forward any surplus monies to the mortgagor.

(d)   Advance secured against the security of the policy is repayable on demand.

(e)   Law of Property Act 1925, ss.93 and 103 are excluded.

(f)   An undertaking by the mortgagor to comply with the terms and conditions of the policy, to pay the premiums on the due dates, and to provide premium receipts to the bank. If the mortgagor fails to do so, the bank is entitled to pay the premiums and debit the borrower's account.

(g)   The bank has a power to exercise its rights and deal with the policy without the borrower's consent.

4.8 MONITORING THE SECURITY

1. *Premiums*   Through monthly diary notes, ensure premiums are paid. Where payment is by standing order or direct debit, check also on a yearly basis that all outstanding premiums are paid. If payment by direct debit or standing order is not made, the latest premium receipts must be checked monthly and yearly. In case of an industrial policy, check the premium receipt book.

2. *Surrender Value*   Where the bank is relying on the surrender value, write to the company on a yearly basis to check the surrender value.

3. *Maturity diary*   Make a diary note of important events, i.e. maturity, at least a month ahead, to ensure that appropriate procedure on the due date is followed.

4.9 RELEASE

The procedure for release will depend upon the type of charge that was originally taken.

4.9.1 Legal assignment

1. When the security is no longer required, then the reassignment which is normally incorporated on the reverse of the assignment form must be completed by the bank, by endorsing a form of discharge by deed.

   Different clauses will be printed for reassignment on a direct form of charge and on the third party security form.

2. If the bank does not have a notice of subsequent charge, return the discharged life policy and previous charges or reassignments to the customer against receipt.

3. If the bank is on notice of a subsequent assignment, forward the policy to the subsequent assignee.

4. In both cases give notice of release to the assurance company.

4.9.2 Equitable assignment

The bank is not required to reassign the policy or endorse receipt when the security is vacated.

1. Mark 'cancelled' on the memorandum of deposit.

2. Return the policy and the cancelled memorandum of deposit to the assignor against the receipt.

3. Give notice of release to the assurance company.

4.10 REALISATION OF A LIFE POLICY

Before realising the life policy ensure that the bank's power of sale has arisen. If a Consumer Credit Act policy, necessary notices are required to be served. Enforcement of the policy will depend upon whether the mortgage is legal or equitable (and in the latter case whether it is under hand or executed by deed, accompanied by an irrevocable power of attorney).

4.11 DEATH

4.11.1 Legal assignment

1. If a bank receives notice of the assured's death, then the account must be stopped and the mandate cancelled.
2. Ask for a certified copy of the death certificate from the deceased's personal representatives.
3. Obtain from the insurance company its form of receipt and claim form, in order to claim the benefit under the policy.
4. Once the receipt is received, send the completed claim form, executed receipt, policy, previous released assignments, bonus notices, charge form and certified copy of death certificate to the company.
5. Make a diary note for receipt of monies.
6. The company will send the cheque, for the amount due, to the bank.
7. Credit the amount to the deceased's account and release the surplus to his personal representatives upon sight of death certificate or letters of administration.
8. If the amount received is less than the total outstanding debt, it should be credited to the securities realised suspense account.

4.11.2 Equitable assignment

1. Upon the assignor's death, write to the executors or personal representatives to forward the proceeds.
2. When the claim form and necessary documents from the company are received, arrange the receipt to be signed by the bank and by the personal representatives or executors.
3. Make sure you advise the assurance company to send the proceeds direct to the bank.
4. If the personal representatives or executors do not co-operate, obtain a court order for sale. This will be time consuming and expensive (unless memorandum of deposit executed by deed with irrevocable power of attorney is held).

4.12 MATURITY

A diary note will alert the bank a few days before the maturity of the policy, so that necessary forms are obtained from the company and lodged before the maturity date.

If the bank is not relying on the security, then discharge and release the deed and forward the policy to the assured against his receipt.

4.12.1 Legal assignment

1. Send the receipt, completed claim form, life policy, bank deed (do not discharge the reassignment), prior discharged assignments, and bonus notices to the assurance company before the maturity date.
2. Diarise for the receipt of monies.
3. When the monies are received, credit the customer's account and advise him.

4.12.2 Equitable assignment

1. The same procedure as above is followed, but the form of receipt will also be required to be signed by the beneficiary.
2. If the beneficiary does not co-operate, obtain a court order (unless memorandum of deposit by deed with irrevocable power of attorney is held).

4.13 SURRENDER

4.13.1 Legal assignment

1. If the customer agrees to surrender the policy, obtain his written confirmation authorising the bank to do this, and written instructions from him to the company to forward the necessary forms.
2. Write to the insurance company to ascertain the surrender value, the reversionary bonus to the last declaration and if premiums are paid up to date.
3. If the mortgagor does not co-operate, under the bank's mortgage it has express authority to surrender the policy at any time without the mortgagor's authority.
4. Check that the assured's age is admitted, the premiums paid, policy is issued and payable in the UK in sterling, that the bank's executed form is properly completed, and that prior assignments or reassignments are held.
5. Obtain a receipt form from the insurance company to be executed by the bank, and advise them of the bank's intention to surrender.
6. Give the mortgagor opportunity and time by a letter, to redeem by discharging the amount.
7. If he does not, send the mortgage deed, an executed receipt, prior released

assignment and reassignments, and bonus notices to the policy to the assurance company advising them to forward the monies direct to the bank.

8.   Diarise receipt of the monies.

9.   If the bank decides to sell the policy, follow the procedure as in 4.14.

4.13.2   Equitable assignment

The bank will need a court order before it can obtain sums under the policy, if memorandum of deposit is not by deed.

If the mortgagor does not sign the surrender papers, reference to the court will involve additional expense, and the surrender value will decrease if premiums are not paid.

If the sum assured and the surrender value are likely to realise a better value, ask the insurance company if they will make the payment of surrender value to the bank against an indemnity. Some companies may agree to this, and it will save time and the costs of application to the court in respect of small amounts.

4.14   SALE OF THE POLICY

4.14.1   Legal assignment

1.   The bank may, at any time, if it wishes, at an agreed consideration, surrender the policy by selling and transferring it to another assignee, but this action is only taken rarely, usually as a last measure.

2.   Consider whether it would be more profitable to sell or to surrender. Many companies purchase life policies and the purchase price may be more than the surrender value.

3.   Check that the bank form provides for the power of sale. Most bank forms exclude s.103 of the Law of Property Act and allow the bank to sell the policy at any time.

4.   If a policy is to be sold at an auction, premiums must be paid up to the date at the time of sale. The bank is entitled to debit the customer's account for payment of premium.

5.   If the bank decides to sell the policy, check:

(a)   The bank has power to sell. Give notice to the trustee or supervisor if the assignor is bankrupt or has executed a mortgage or entered into an individual voluntary arrangement.

(b)   The assignor's background of health and age before deciding to sell, and write to the assignor providing time to discharge the amount due.

(c)   If the amount is not discharged, send the policy and assignment, details of surrender value, premiums, bonuses and prior assignment, and reassignments to the bank's agents to sell.

(d)   The reserve price is indicated to the agents.

(e)   For direct security, apply sale proceeds in reduction of the debt. If third party, credit to the securities realised account.

(f)   If any surplus is available, enquire from the insurance company whether they have notice of subsequent mortgagees. If there are subsequent mortgagees, send the surplus to them, otherwise send them to the mortgagor.

4.15   CONVERSION INTO PAID UP POLICY

If the customer is not able to pay the premiums, ask him to contact the assurance company to issue a paid up policy for a smaller sum, in substitution for the existing policy, so that the surrender value is maintained.

4.16   LOAN BY COMPANY AGAINST POLICY

A mortgagor can sometimes obtain a loan from the insurance company against the surrender value of the policy.

If the surrender value is more than the amount of loan from the insurance company, it may repay or reduce the bank's borrowing, thus maintaining the capital value. In this case, the bank should enter into a priority agreement with the customer and the insurance company, and retain the mortgage as a second charge. In due course, when the insurance company loan is repaid, the surrender value will increase. The bank should:

(a)   hold the loan agreement signed by the customer (undated);
(b)   obtain a letter from the customer authorising the loan money to be paid to the bank.

4.17   LIFE POLICY UNDER CONSUMER CREDIT ACT 1974

Do not accept a third party security to secure a regulated borrowing. Instead take a guarantee from the non-borrowing chargor to secure the principal debtor's liability. If tangible security is taken to support the guarantee, a first party (direct) charge form should be taken.

5 LAND

5.1 LEGAL ESTATES IN LAND

According to s.1 Law of Property Act 1925, the two legal estates which may be created over land (with a maximum of four legal owners) are:

(a) Freehold ownership
Known as 'fee simple absolute in possession' but subject to certain restrictions, e.g. Town & Country Planning Acts. Ownership is retained by the title holders until the land is sold, or until such owner(s) die. This title can be subject only to legislation and restrictive covenants.

(b) Leasehold ownership
Known as 'a term of years absolute'. A legal estate in leasehold land created from the freehold estate by the freeholder (landlord), comprising a lease for a stated term of years in favour of the lessee. Upon expiry of the term of years, the title reverts back to the freeholder. (Since 1967 a leaseholder has had a statutory right in certain circumstances to compel the sale to him of the freehold reversion. See the Leasehold Reform Housing and Urban Development Act 1993.)

5.2 EQUITABLE ESTATES IN LAND

Two types of equitable estates are:

(a) freehold: estate for life and estate in fee tail;
(b) leasehold: estate which is not for a term of years absolute.

5.3 UNREGISTERED LAND

Under the Land Registration Act 1925 all land in England and Wales is to be registered at HM Land Registry.

Until land is registered it is referred to as an unregistered land, and the title or ownership is evidenced by a bundle of deeds. These deeds must include a good root of title, a holding deed and a chain of title linking the two. The bundle of deeds may contain abstracts or epitomes of title which are a summary of documents reciting past events, and are sometimes certified by solicitors, e.g. conveyances, births, deaths, marriages, wills affecting the title. They are prepared and certified by solicitors when documents covering these transactions are missing from the deed.

5.3.1 Various documents of title for unregistered land

The chain of documents to title would include:

1. Conveyance: the deed by which freehold title to land is transferred to a purchaser for consideration, on the date shown.
2. Lease: the deed by which leasehold title is created.
3. Assignment: the deed by which leasehold interest is transferred.
4. Deed of gift: transfer for no consideration. Banks should be careful regarding possible insolvency. Deeds could be declared void if the donor becomes insolvent within five years, or, at any time, if it was found that the donor intended to defraud the creditors.
5. Assent: transfer of title by the personal representatives of deceased person(s).
6. Holding deed: the deed that transferred the title of the land to the present owner.
7. Good root of title: A document at least 15 years old showing undoubted title to the land.
8. Chain of title: All the deeds and documents from the good root of title to the holding deed with no obvious breaks between them.

5.4 REGISTERED LAND

There are various District Registries of the Land Registry in the country. Registration is compulsory in all areas but only when certain events take place.

Each plot of land is allocated a title number on registration. Following registration the title deeds are replaced by:

(a) a land certificate: issued to owners when no legal mortgages are outstanding;

(b) a charge certificate: when a legal mortgage is registered the Land Registry retains the land certificate and a charge certificate is issued to each mortgagee.

The old bundle of title deeds will accompany the land certificate or the first charge certificate to be issued, and are then known as pre-registration deeds and documents.

The land certificate or charge certificate contains three registers which are:

69

(a)　the property register – contains a description of the property and states whether freehold or leasehold;

(b)　the proprietorship register – describes the name(s) of the owner(s) and the type of title granted, i.e. absolute (freehold or leasehold); good leasehold; possessory; qualified;

(c)　the charges register – shows any encumbrances of the title, for example, mortgages, restrictive covenants, notices under Matrimonial Homes Act 1957 and 1983.

Plan of area clearly identifying property included in the title number will be attached.

5.5　GENERAL CONSIDERATIONS BEFORE TAKING UNREGISTERED AND REGISTERED LAND AS SECURITY

Before incurring costs for completing the security, make preliminary enquiries and searches to ascertain the bank's priority, ensure that sufficient margin is available, and that the security has a good root of title so that there are no problems for realisation. Considerations listed below should be borne in mind.

5.5.1　Searches

The following searches must be made.

1.　Land Registry search (for registered land)
This search at the appropriate District Land Registry will reveal entries recorded in the property, proprietorship and the charges register.

2.　Local Land Charges register
These are charges against the property. Search at the relevant local authority that there are no adverse entries on the register which will affect the value of the property as security.

3.　Company searches
If the property is charged by a company make a search at Companies Registry:

(a)　to establish if a prior charge has been created;
(b)　that the company has not registered a debenture, in favour of another bank, which contains a *pari passu* clause (negative pledge);
(c)　that the company has not been dissolved or 'struck off', or an administrative receiver or a liquidator appointed.

4. Searching at the Land Charges Registry (for unregistered land)

This search, made against a person, will reveal any charges recorded against that person. Official searches show the rights, if any, of third parties enforceable against the land and charges recorded against the title holder's name.

Procedure

The procedure for searching is as follows:

(i) Ascertain the owners, and search in the correct names and spellings of the owners, as Land Charges Department maintains registers of names and not of properties.

(ii) If the land is owned by trustees, partners or joint owners search against the names of all of them.

(iii) Search against the names of all owners since the date of the transaction, which constitutes the root of title, to ensure that charges against previous owners are not outstanding. Some institutions as a practice search against all legal mortgagees since 1926 (except banks and building societies), to check if in cases where the mortgagee has sub-mortgaged, the sub-mortgagee's interest in land has not been retained, even when the owner of the land may have paid off his liability under the mortgage.

(iv) Complete form K15 and send it to the Land Charges Department. This form will secure an official search for all registers (A, B, C, D, E and F) kept at Land Charges Department. For details of these registers refer to pages 82–84.

(v) If a search reveals a C(i) charge or a C(iii) charge, depending on whether the mortgage revealed by the search is legal or equitable, the bank will have a third mortgage. In other words, the first mortgagee will have the title deeds. The second mortgagee with a legal charge will register a puisne mortgage C(i) charge or, if an equitable mortgage, then a C(iii) charge will be registered.

(vi) Registration of class F charge would mean that the charge has been effected as a right of occupation within the provisions of the Matrimonial Homes Act 1983.

(vii) If a search reveals class D charge, this will be due to the breach of the restrictive covenants in respect of business premises.

When to search

The timing of searches will depend on the type of facility given.

(a) Loan Account

Carry out the search before the execution of the mortgage form. In case of a second or subsequent charge (according to the Land Charges Act 1972), register the mortgage on form K1 within 15 days from the date of the search certificate. This will give protection against the entries made in the intervening period between the date of the search certificate and the date of the execution, except for an entry subject to a 'priority notice' on the register before the issuance of the certificate. The certificate will show the date of expiry of the priority period.

(b)   Overdraft

Make a search on or after the date the mortgage has been executed, so that a lender making further advances by way of overdraft will have protection from subsequent mortgages registered, either from the date of his mortgage or date of his search, whichever occurred last. The bank will not be affected by any intervening entries: s.94 (2) Law of Property Act 1925.

Where more than one mortgage is given by the customer, determine the bank's priority.

Whether the mortgage is legal or equitable, a legal mortgagee cannot obtain priority by taking a legal mortgage.

5.5.2   Priorities

Priorities are determined by whichever comes first, either possession of the title deeds with no notice of other interests at that time, or the date of registration of a charge at Land Charges Department (s.97 Law of Property Act 1925 and Land Charges Act 1972 s.4(5)).

Because the first mortgagee will be in possession of title deeds, it is not necessary to register at the Land Charges Department.

If the second mortgagee fails to register its charge and the third mortgagee registers before it, then whether the mortgage is legal or equitable, the date of registration as a land charge will determine the priority (s. 97 of the Law of Property Act 1925). Therefore the third mortgagee will rank ahead of the second mortgagee, even if the third mortgagee was on actual notice of the second mortgage when it acquired its interest (s.199(1) Law of Property Act 1925).

If both the second and third mortgagees fail to register, the second mortgagee's charge is void as against the third mortgagee for want of registration, and the third mortgagee will rank ahead of the second mortgagee: i.e. the last will rank first (s.4(5) Land Charges Act 1972).

5.5.3   Valuation

1.   Arrange for the property to be valued by an officer or estate agent in

accordance with the lender's practice. For specialised commercial properties it is advisable that it is valued by a professional valuer or surveyor.

According to the Building Society Rules, building society valuations should not be undertaken by their officers or employees involved in making advances or assessments, or by a person introducing the account or receiving commission, or by any person who has financial interest in the sale of the property. Building societies valuations are usually carried out by the surveyors.

Value will depend on the condition of the property, access, location, local authority planning (e.g. development or building of roads), its terms of occupation, whether it is leasehold or freehold, commercial or residential, owner occupied or tenanted, and if the parties with equitable or overriding interests have executed a deed postponing their interests in favour of the bank.

2.　Check the local search to ascertain that the property is not subject to a local authority grant as this will affect the bank's security.

3.　Consider the chances of selling the property if the lender takes possession.

4.　Ensure that the property offered as security is the property being charged. Where necessary identify the property and send a copy of the plan with the area being charged edged and marked to the valuer.

5.　Some banks also forward to the valuer a signed memorandum from the owner revealing details of other occupants. The valuer is asked to reaffirm if during his internal inspection the occupancy appeared to be as stated. The bank can then obtain necessary postponement of their interests in favour of the bank. If any tenancy not disclosed on the memorandum is revealed then the property is to be valued accordingly. Valuers owe a duty of care to a third party relying on their valuation and in *Singer and Friedlander Ltd* v *John D. Wood & Co.* [1977], the valuers were held liable to the plaintiff merchant bank for considerable over-valuation. In *Smith* v *Eric S. Bush (a firm)* [1989], the House of Lords held that a disclaimer of liability by a surveyor valuing a house for a building society was ineffective because it was not reasonable under the Unfair Contract Terms Act 1977.

If a leasehold property is offered as security ensure the following:

(a)　If the lease incorporates a clause whereby the landlord has a right to re-enter upon bankruptcy or liquidation, ask the valuer to value the property subject to this clause, bearing in mind that upon the occurrence of these events the goodwill of the business will be lost.

(b)　Send a copy of the lease to the valuer so that he can value the property subject to the terms and conditions, covenants, rent reviews, ground rent and unexpired term. A commercial property will be valued on the basis of its turnover. For a tenanted property a copy of the tenancy agreement needs to be obtained so that the property can be valued subject to the rental income, and in accordance with the provisions of the Rent Acts if it falls under such provisions.

6. If further advances are made arrange for a new valuation (depending on the lenders' practice).

If a charge over farmland is taken, a charge under the Agricultural Holdings Act 1948 will rank in priority to an existing mortgage and the bank will not be able to evict a tenant of agricultural land.

7. After the receipt of valuation, if the valuer's report suggests any essential repairs, obtain an undertaking from the borrower to carry out these repairs within a specified time limit. Arrange a subsequent inspection to ensure that they are carried out. If major repairs are to be undertaken, retain some of the advance and only release the amount after they are carried out to the lender's satisfaction.

5.5.4 Property in sole name or joint names

Ascertain if the property charged is held by the registered proprietors as joint tenants or as tenants in common.

1. *Joint tenancy (e.g. husband and wife)*
If the co-owners own the property jointly, on death of one, the share passes to the survivor(s).

In case of a joint tenancy, the lender should not worry about the joint tenants' proportionate rights. The lender will not require the security to be re-charged, although under the trust which the joint tenants hold for one another, there will exist an equitable interest instead of a legal interest.

If only one of the two joint tenants signs the charge, care must be taken as the other party may have refused to sign. Even where both appear to have signed, the signature may be forged.

In such cases, one party signing the form will affect the joint tenancy, which will convert the registered holders into tenants in common, thus creating an equitable charge over the beneficial interest in future sale proceeds of the property: *First National Securities Ltd* v *Hegarty* [1984].

2. *Tenancy in common*
Each partner has a specific share in the equity of the property. On the death of one partner, the deceased's share forms part of the estate.

5.5.5 Investigation of title for unregistered land

1. Banks usually consider it unnecessary to carry out a report on title, particularly where a first mortgagee is a reputable professional lender, e.g. a bank or a building society. Obtain the title deeds, if a first mortgage. Title deeds consist of a number of documents forming a chain of title, showing previous dealings and transfers in the land, which make up the title to unregistered land.
2. Check the deeds against the schedule or send it to the solicitors (in accordance with the bank's practice), and ensure no documents are missing. Examine to see that customer has a good root of title, i.e. the deeds should show a chain of title and previous sales, released mortgages, local and land charges searches and transfers going back at least 15 years.

Note: An equitable mortgage, and a general devise of land, are not considered a good root of title. If a testator died before 1926, then a specific devise, and if after 1925, then the written assent of the personal representatives, are good root of title, although a mortgagor or a purchaser must check probate to ensure there are no endorsements.

The lender must also abstract legal mortgages even if discharged and discharged equitable mortgages.

3. Finally, check that all the documents have been properly executed by the persons named therein and properly stamped. Ensure that property has been appropriately described.
4. For an unregistered land offered as security, always apply for an official search of the index map of registered titles on Land Registry form 96 to ascertain if the land has been registered.

5.5.6 Investigation of title for registered land

Title to registered land is evidenced by a land certificate. If the legal title, freehold or leasehold, is subject to a first legal mortgage, then it is determined by searching at the relevant District Land Registry. (For details see pages 96–98.)

5.5.7 Matrimonial home

Registering an interest
1. Whether the property is registered, or unregistered the Matrimonial Homes Act 1983 (MHA) gives a spouse protection of right of occupation by registering an equitable charge. This charge is registered at a Land Charges Registry as a class F charge (if unregistered land) and a 'notice' at the appropriate District Land Registry (if registered land). Such a 'notice' defeats the purchaser or mortgagee, unless written waiver of priority is obtained by the purchaser or mortgagee.

2. If an MHA charge is not registered then, for registered and unregistered land, the wife will have an equitable interest if she is in actual occupation, has also contributed financially towards the cost of the property and has some proprietory interest: *Hodgson v Marks* [1971]; *Winkworth v Edward Baron Development Co. Ltd* [1987]. This charge is an overriding interest which may be held by anyone, not just a wife. Also, because a wife has an MHA interest, it does not follow that she has an overriding interest: *Caunce v Caunce* [1969].

3. Even if the spouse has no legal title in the matrimonial home, and whether the land is registered or unregistered, these problems may arise because of existence of the following:

(a) *With unregistered land*
   (i) Equitable interests, e.g. class F charge is registered at Land Charges Department in respect of Matrimonial Homes Act.
   (ii) Equitable rights of occupation, irrespective of any registration; e.g. by occupation of the spouse who does not own the property but occupies it and may have contributed towards the purchase price or payments for mortgage: *Kingsnorth Trust Ltd v Tizard* [1986].

(b) *With registered land*
   (i) Equitable interests, e.g. 'notice' registered at Land Registry in respect of Matrimonial Homes Act.
   (ii) Overriding interests (which are unregistrable); e.g. the rights of an occupant to remain in occupation (s.70(1)(g) Land Registration Act 1925).
   (iii) Minor interests, registered at Land Registry: *Midland Bank Ltd v Dobson* [1985]; *Winkworth v Edward Baron Development Co. Ltd* [1987].

5.5.8   Overriding interests

Overriding interests are unregistrable, but are binding on a person who acquires an interest in land; e.g. by purchase (which includes mortgages). Interests such as leases for less than 21 years and legal easements; e.g. rights of way, are overriding interests.

Banks should inspect the property and enquire the present occupancy at the time of creation of a charge: *Hodgson v Marks* [1971].

Rights of persons in actual occupation of the property, or those receiving rents and profits, are protected by the Land Registration Act 1925, s. 70(1)(g). In order to obtain protection under the Act, actual occupation as well as proprietory rights must exist; e.g. a wife will have an overriding interest if she is in actual occupation (which gives constructive notice of her beneficial interest) and has contributed towards cost of the house: *Williams & Glyn's Bank Ltd v Boland* [1981]; *Williams & Glyn's Bank Ltd* v *Brown* [1981].

Problems of overriding interests arise with registered land. If the land is not registered then the problem of 'constructive notice' arises.

If the cohabitee who is an equitable owner consents to the legal proprietor's mortgage then he/she will not gain priority over a legal mortgagee: *Bristol and West Building Society* v *Henning and another* [1985].

If the bank is offered a security of a matrimonial home, where one spouse is the owner, the following actions are required:

1. According to the Land Registration Act, 1925, s.70(1)(g), it is important to ascertain actual occupation at the relevant time and date of registration or creation of the mortgage: *Abbey National Building Society* v *Cann* [1990]. If the bank is aware of the spouse's occupation and fails to investigate anything suspicious, it will be deemed to have a constructive notice: *Kingsnorth Trust Ltd* v *Tizard* [1986]. Also enquire if other people are occupying the property.

In the case of registered land, if the wife has a financial interest, enquire if the interest is of a kind which might give rise to an equitable interest in the property and an overriding interest under s.70(1)(g) of the Land Registration Act 1925.

In the case of unregistered land, a spouse's Matrimonial Homes Act 1983 charge is not effective unless it is registered as a class F charge at the Land Charges Registry. This will give notice and defeat the mortgagee or prospective purchaser unless they obtain a waiver or letter of postponement from that spouse. A house owned in joint names is not necessarily owned in equal shares by the spouses: *Young* v *Young* [1984].

In the case of both registered and unregistered land, if a spouse has not registered Matrimonial Homes Act charge, then unless the spouse can show that he or she has an equitable interest by contributing financially towards purchase or improvement: *Midland Bank Ltd* v *Dobson* [1985]; *Midland Bank Ltd* v *Farm Pride Hatcheries Ltd* [1980], with the intention from the proprietor of acquiring some property interest: *Hodgson* v *Marks* [1971]; *Pascoe* v *Turner* [1979]; *Winkworth* v *Edward Baron Development Co. Ltd* [1987], the spouse cannot register an equitable interest as a land charge, as it is a trust for sale incapable of registration. The lender's rights will be affected if there is an actual or constructive notice of the spouse's rights, or if the spouse has authority to bind the other spouse.

The principles of *Boland's* case depend on the circumstances of each particular case, e.g. *City of London Building Society* v *Flegg & Others* [1986];

Midland Bank Ltd v *Dobson* [1985]; *Lloyds Bank plc* v *Rossett* [1990]; *Abbey National Building Society* v *Cann* [1990]; *Winkworth* v *Edward Baron Development Co. Ltd* [1987]; *Midland Bank Ltd* v *Farm Pride Hatcheries Ltd* [1980].

2.   Enquire if the land is registered, unregistered, tenanted, long or short lease, or if it is the matrimonial home to determine the extent of equitable and overriding interests of the spouse. If the husband has acquired an interest in the dwelling house for value, the wife's right of occupation cannot be effective against him unless it is registered. Overriding interests do not arise only by virtue of occupation.

If there is more than one matrimonial home, the wife can only protect her right of occupation for the one she occupies or intends to occupy.

3.   Carry out a voters' roll search to reaffirm the occupancy.

4.   After the details of occupancies have been ascertained, obtain a signed memorandum from the owner or prospective buyer, detailing names of all the occupants over the age of 18, names of all persons who have contributed towards cost or purchase, and confirmation if the vendor has been paid in full or not. Obtain from those occupants having an interest a waiver postponing their interest in favour of the mortgagee.

Some banks send the signed memorandum from the owner detailing the occupancy to the valuer, so that when internal valuation of the property is made these details can be verified.

5.   If the search reveals an entry recorded at the Land Charges Department (class F if unregistered land or a 'notice' at Land Registry if registered land), by a spouse who is not the registered proprietor, obtain a waiver from the spouse postponing his or her interest. Also confirm that the bank's charge will have priority over the spouse's interest. Otherwise the bank will have difficulty in obtaining vacant possession when selling the property, thus affecting its security. If a bank obtains a charge on a property executed by one spouse without obtaining consent or charging of interest of the other spouse, its security will be affected: *Williams & Glyn's Bank Ltd* v *Boland* [1981]; *Williams & Glyn's Bank Ltd* v *Brown* [1981].

6.   To protect against such prior equitable interests, when a mortgage is taken on the matrimonial home, ask the spouse who is not the registered owner to join in executing the mortgage form. In this way the spouse agrees to charge his or her interest and postpone the rights, including rights of occupation, in favour of the bank.

Note: If the spouse (owner) deserts his or her partner, the lender can accept repayments from the non-owning partner (s.1(5) Matrimonial Homes Act).

If the facts suggest that the wife allowed the husband to mortgage the house because this was the only way of refinancing the purchase, the husband is deemed to have acted as an agent. Therefore the mortgagees' interests will take priority.

The third party will only be bound if he or she has actual or constructive notice, or if the wife was 'in actual occupation' at the relevant time of registration.

5.5.9 Undue influence

1. If a mortgage over a house in joint names of husband and wife is offered as security, or if the non-owning spouse has an overriding interest, or if the other occupant guarantees the loan or joins in the mortgage, the spouse cannot claim undue influence unless it can be shown that he or she has suffered a manifest and unfair disadvantage. The bank, however, should not exercise undue influence in obtaining the joint owner's signature to the document: *National Westminster Bank plc* v *Morgan* [1985].
2. Do not give documents to another interested party, e.g. a husband who needs the facility. Ensure that there is no undue influence or misrepresentation, and that opportunity to seek independent legal advice is given. The implications of decisions in the cases of *Barclays Bank plc* v *O'Brien* [1993], *CIBC Mortgages plc* v *Pitt and Another* [1993] and *Bank of Credit and Commerce International SA* v *Aboody* [1989] should be considered. Also relevant are *Kingsnorth Trust Ltd* v *Bell* [1986], *Avon Finance Co Ltd* v *Bridger* [1985] and *Cornish* v *Midland Bank plc* [1985].

In respect of lending by the building societies, if a spouse has registered his or her rights under the Matrimonial Homes Act 1983, it is regarded as a class 2 loan (Building Societies Act 1986).

For a spouse to acquire the rights under the Matrimonial Homes Act 1983, the spouse must be in occupation before the execution of the mortgage: *Abbey National Building Society* v *Cann* [1990].

5.5.10 Other considerations

1. *Purpose of the loan*: Enquire the purpose of the loan (i.e. residential, or commercial), income, other financial commitments of the borrower and the number of dependants.
2. *Minors*: Ensure that the borrower is not a minor: Minors Contracts Act 1987; Law of Property Act s.1(6).
3. *Limited companies (as regards building societies):* Under the Building Societies Act 1986 loans to limited companies are class 2 loans. They must

ensure that their lending is limited to 25% of the commercial assets of a building society.

4. *Executors and administrators (as regards building societies):* Although loans to executors and administrators can be regarded as suitable security, in respect of building society loans, borrowing members are liable for their debts. Personal representatives may not be personally liable and powers of consolidation may not exist.

Most lenders also make loans to housing associations. They fall under class 2 loans for building society lending.

5. *Mental incapacity or bankruptcy:* Make sure that the borrower is not of unsound mind or an undischarged bankrupt. Most lenders make a bankruptcy search on form K16 before lending.

6. *Legal or equitable:* Decide whether a legal mortgage or an equitable mortgage is to be taken and bear in mind the advantages of a legal mortgage as opposed to that of an equitable one.

7. *Insurance (as regards building societies):* The guidelines listed below which are set out by the Building Societies Association in accordance with the recommendations of the Office of Fair Trading should be followed.

They should not stipulate use of a particular insurance company with which the society has an agency.

Existing borrowers should be allowed to change their insurance to

(a)   any of the main insurers of the society; or

(b)   agree for the society to arrange the cover, provided its terms and conditions, amount and services are satisfactory and meet the society's requirements; or

(c)   allow the borrower to arrange the insurance himself through another broker (not the society's) provided the above conditions (a) and (b) are met and the borrower undertakes to pay the premiums regularly to keep the society covered and not to effect change in the terms of the policy without the society's approval.

In the case of new borrowers, the procedure outlined below should be followed.

Any one of the three insurance companies proposed by the society may be chosen, but the borrower should be allowed to effect insurance with any other insurer. Where the society arranges the cover, the same procedures as detailed for existing borrowers in (a) to (b) are to be followed.

Most building societies' policies are arranged in the joint names of the lender and the mortgagor so that the claim will be paid in joint names. In the case of leasehold property, if it is not a condition of a lease that the insurance will be effected by the landlord, the lender will arrange freeholder's interest to be noted on the policy.

5.6 FIRST LEGAL MORTGAGE OF UNREGISTERED FREEHOLD OR LEASEHOLD LAND

5.6.1 Taking the security

By s. 85 of the Law of Property Act 1925, a legal mortgage is now created in two ways:

(a) by a lease of land for a term of years, subject to a proviso for cesser of the term on redemption (a term of 3,000 years is suggested);

(b) by a charge by deed expressed to be by way of legal mortgage.

Some of the steps outlined below have already been discussed in greater depth in section 5.5, and are therefore not discussed in detail in this section.

1. Investigation of title

Obtain the title deeds. Check that the property offered as security is in fact the one being charged and that the customer has a good root of title.

Where a customer is not able to lodge title deeds, the bank is on constructive notice that there is a prior charge.

If it is difficult to investigate the title, send the deeds to the bank's solicitors against their undertaking. Ask them to prepare a report on title, confirming the customer has a good root of title, and drawing attention to any onerous covenants or defects affecting the title.

2. Valuation

Arrange for the valuation to be carried out in accordance with the bank's practice.

(a) Check that legislation, e.g. the Rent Acts which give security of tenure relating to furnished lettings, does not affect the property.

(b) If a council property is charged, establish if any improvement grants have been given and if so, whether this is likely to affect the property.

(c) Enquire with the local authority concerning planning regulations or development plans, and if the property is subject to a compulsory purchase order.

3. Occupancy

(a)   Check and enquire the present occupancy of the property being charged i.e. owner occupied or tenanted. Ask the owner to sign a memorandum detailing occupancy. The bank's mortgage will be subject to the rights of prior occupation of the tenants, if the property is tenanted at the time when the mortgage is executed: *Universal Permanent Building Society* v *Cooke* [1951]. Decisions in *Williams & Glyn's* v *Boland* and other cases, and the effect of Matrimonial Homes Act 1983 discussed earlier, must be considered.

(b)   If a person who is not an owner of the property, contributed towards its purchase and is in occupation of that property when it is mortgaged to the bank, obtain a waiver from that person. Otherwise the person will have rights which override the bank's mortgage rights to vacant possession, even if a class F charge has not been registered at the Land Charges Registry.

The problems arising as a result of misrepresentation, undue influence, and failure to give an opportunity for independent legal advice at the time of execution of these waivers or a charge should be considered. Similar considerations for occupancy for a property charged by a limited company should be given.

4. Land Charges Searches and Bankruptcy Searches

(a)   If the lender is uncertain as to whether any freehold or leasehold land or a rent charge is registered, or if any priority notices or cautions against first registration have been recorded, apply on form 96 for an official search of the index map. The full postal address must be given on the form, failing which a copy of a plan must be submitted.

(b)   Apply on form K16 ('bankruptcy only' search) to ascertain the solvency of a potential borrower who is not yet recorded on the register of title at the Local Land Registry.

(c)   To ensure that no prior mortgage, interest or encumbrance exists, which will affect the property, apply for a search on form K15 at the Land Charges Registry before the mortgage is executed. The search should be against the name of the mortgagor at all known addresses.

The Land Charges Department will reply on form K17, if there are no mortgages or encumbrances, with a reply 'no subsisting entries'. In this case arrange for the mortgage to be executed within 15 days from the date of the search and before the end of expiry period shown on the search.

If any entries are recorded against the owner(s), the reply of the official search will be on form K18. It will show the date of the certificate and the date when the protection period ends.

If further information is required relating to entries shown on form K18, send form K19 to obtain office copies from the Land Charges Department. These will reveal full details of the entries.

For 'bankruptcy only' searches, certificates of the result of the search are also issued on forms K17 and K18.

(d)   Search again on the date the mortgage is executed if lending is on the current account.

Registers at the Land Charges Department show entries relating to pending actions in bankruptcy, liquidation (petition, writs, bankruptcy order, winding up orders, charging orders, judgment creditor), annuities and Deeds of Arrangement.

Land charges are divided into class registers: A, B, C, D, E and F. The following classes are important to lenders:

(a)   Class C includes:
    (i)   C(i) – Puisne mortgage – is a legal mortgage or a legal estate where mortgagees are not in possession of the title deeds. Puisne mortgages are therefore mainly second or third mortgages, with a first mortgagee who will not need to register.
    (ii)   C(ii) – A limited owner's charge – an equitable charge acquired by a tenant for life or other statutory owner by discharging certain liabilities, e.g. death duties.
    (iii)   C(iii) – General equitable charge – an equitable charge not protected by deposit of title deeds. It may be registered within the 15 days priority period by obtaining an official search certificate. Section 2 of the Law of Property (Miscellaneous Provisions) Act 1989 repealed s.40 of the Law of Property Act 1925. It sets out new rules regarding dispositions of interests in land, thus making the equitable doctrine of part performance unenforceable.
    (iv)   C(iv) – Estate contracts – relate to contracts which create or convey a legal estate, e.g. for the sale of land or an option to purchase the freehold interest or renew a lease. Prior to the new

rule, s.2 of the Law of Property (Miscellaneous Provisions) Act 1989 coming into force, an option contract of sale made by a deed was registered as a c(iv) charge (in the case of unregistered land) at the Land Charges Registry, or by notice of a minor interest (in the case of registered land) at the Land Registry. This procedure is no longer valid, because according to s.2 of the new Act, all contracts must be signed by both parties and made by way of a single document incorporating all the terms of the agreement.

(b)   Class D includes charges in favour of the Inland Revenue relating to capital transfer or inheritance tax; and restrictive covenants restricting use of the land and equitable easement, e.g. right of way.

(c)   Class F includes charges affecting matrimonial homes by virtue of the Matrimonial Homes Act 1983. Under this Act the rights of occupation given to a spouse are a charge on the estate and this charge can be registrable.

5. Local Land Charges Search
These are charges registered against the land in the appropriate local authority's register.

(a)   Search to check that there are no adverse entries, e.g. restrictions on the user of the land, road widening or motorway construction plans, planning permissions or compulsory purchase orders, which may adversely affect the property thus making it difficult to sell later.

(b)   Where monies are lent to effect any material change in the use of the property or for making alterations, check that prior written consent of the local authority exists, and the business is carried on according to the authorised use by the council. Non-compliance with council requirements will force them to serve an enforcement notice for breach of its conditions, thus affecting goodwill and security.

(c)   If lending is against the security of a plot of vacant land, search at the local authority register of common land to ascertain if any rights have been registered: *G&K Ladenbau (UK) Ltd* v *Crawley & Dereya* [1978].

6. Execution of mortgage

(a) Establish the legal owner of the property being charged. Ascertain if a property is owned in the sole name of the husband or if it is a joint tenancy or tenancy in common, so that the spouse can be asked where necessary to join in the mortgage.

(b) *Sole proprietorship*: If a married customer charges a property, establish if any party has contributed towards the purchase or upkeep of the house, otherwise their equitable rights will rank in priority to the legal mortgagee's rights: *Williams & Glyn's Bank Ltd* v *Boland* [1981]; *Williams & Glyn's Bank Ltd* v *Brown* [1981]. The decision in *Bristol and West Building Society* v *Henning and Another* [1985] has given some comfort to the financial institutions.

(c) *Joint proprietorship*: If a husband and wife are both charging the property for a loan given in joint names, claims of undue influence are unlikely. But if the property, in joint names of husband and wife, is charged for the husband's borrowing, claims of undue influence are more than likely: *City of London Building Society* v *Flegg & Others* [1986]. If the wife's signature is forged on the mortgage form, the bank will not have a charge on the wife's share: *First National Securities Ltd* v *Hegarty* [1984].

(d) If the mortgage is to be executed at the bank or a branch:
   (i) Use the correct bank mortgage form. Complete all the details. Building societies have different forms for different types of mortgage lendings.
   (ii) In the unregistered section of the form list the last conveyance or assignment or schedule, and list the deeds. Insert the description of the property.
   (iii) Date the mortgage on the day it is executed. If executed by a limited company, see Chapter 6. All mortgage forms are usually witnessed by a bank officer or the mortgagor's solicitor, by adding their signatures as witnesses.

7. Registration

(a) As the first mortgagee will be in possession of the title deeds, it will not need to register the charge at the Land Charges Registry, provided that the bank or building society has carried out a search before the mortgage is executed, and no adverse entries have been revealed.

(b)   If the lender has to part with the deeds, temporarily register a c(i) charge so that the bank's priority against subsequent mortgagees is retained.

(c)   If the mortgage is given by a limited company, register the charge at Companies Registry within 21 days of execution, and follow the procedure given in Chapter 6.

8. Insurance

(a)   Ensure that a policy is taken out from a reputable insurance company for an adequate fire cover up to full reinstatement cost, including architect's and surveyor's costs and other risks. Check that it is in the names of the mortgagors or landlord if required by the lease. For commercial properties, breakage of plate glass, and loss of profits and rents must be covered. For hotels or public houses, the licence must be insured.

(b)   Ask the customer to deposit the policy. To ensure premiums are paid up to date, it is a good practice to arrange a standing order so that the bank can monitor the premiums.

(c)   If a leasehold property is charged, check the clauses in the lease to ascertain who is responsible for the insurance generally, and for specific conditions insuring the landlord's fixtures and fittings, loss of profits, etc. If it is a condition that the landlord will insure and recover the cost of premiums from the owner, obtain a copy of the policy from the landlords or their agents, and give notice of the bank's interest.

Building societies must ensure that insurance is arranged in accordance with the guidelines set out by the society. These are detailed in 5.5.10.

(d)   Give notice to the insurance company in duplicate of the bank's interest and ask them to acknowledge the notice, confirming the bank's interest.

(e)   Make a record in the diary for renewal of premium dates.

9. Further searches
Carry out an official search on the date the mortgage is executed, if lending is on a loan account, and after the date of the mortgage, if it is on an overdraft account.

10.   Leasehold property

Examine the lease to establish:

(a)   If the lessor's consent is required to create any mortgage or assignment, in which case obtain a consent in writing for creation of the mortgage before it is executed. Check that a consent was obtained when assignment took place.

(b)   Who is responsible for the insurance and if a requirement of a particular insurance company is stipulated.

(c)   If a lease contains a provision to forward a copy of the mortgage or assignment to the lessors or their solicitors at the time of giving the notice. In this case send the notice in duplicate, asking them to acknowledge the copy and confirm if the payment of rent is up to date.

(d)   To whom the ground rent is payable. Obtain current ground rent receipt from the customer and ask him to forward all future receipts to the bank. Make a diary note to ensure that future rent receipts are produced.

(e)   Check other clauses and covenants, i.e. covenants to repair, any restriction on underlease or assignment, 'bankruptcy clause'.

(f)   Ascertain the unexpired term of the lease, as value will depend on the unexpired term.

(g)   Check that the head lease, all the assignments forming a root of title, a sublease (if the chargor's title is evidenced by sublease) are all with the title deeds. If the sublease is for less than 15 years, ask for the original lease under which the sublease was granted.

5.7   SECOND LEGAL MORTGAGE OF UNREGISTERED FREEHOLD OR LEASEHOLD LAND

5.7.1   Specific considerations

Apart from the general considerations already discussed, the following should be borne in mind:

(a)   Ensure that the bank has sufficient equity by considering the value of the property and the amount of advance.

(b)   If the first mortgagee decides to sell, he or she will recover capital plus interest. Therefore, in calculating net value, retain a wider margin. In some cases, banks pay off the first mortgagee and take a first charge on the property so that they can control the position.

(c)   On commencement of foreclosure proceedings by first mortgagee, the second mortgage would be extinguished. Although the second mortgagee will be given an option of either paying off the first mortgagee or losing its security, according to the Law of Property Act 1925 s.91(2), the court can direct a sale of property instead of foreclosure at the request of the mortgagor or second mortgagee.

5.7.2   Taking the security

A second mortgage can be created by a charge by way of legal mortgage, or by granting a lease for one day longer than that granted to the first mortgagee.

A second mortgage over a leasehold property can be created by a charge by way of legal mortgage, or by a sublease for a term one day longer than the term granted to the first mortgagee.

Almost the same steps as those for a first mortgage of unregistered land (5.6.1, numbers 2 to 6 and 8 and 9 in the case of freehold land, and number 10 in the case of leasehold land) are to be followed. These steps are therefore only listed below for reference purposes, except for the following amended and additional steps which are explained in more detail.

1. Investigation of title (amended procedure)
The title deeds will be with the first mortgagee, but the second mortgagee must examine the title. If the first mortgagee is a reputable institution, some lenders consider it safe to rely on the first mortgagee's investigation, but request a copy lease or conveyance to examine the clauses.

Some institutions who are second mortgagees request the first mortgagees to send the deeds to their solicitors against their undertaking to hold them to their order for inspection purposes and return. The solicitors then provide a report on title to the second mortgagees.

2. Prior mortgage enquiry (additional procedure)
Send a prior mortgage enquiry form, with the mortgagor's authority to the first mortgagee (usually a standard form for each institution). This form will require the first mortgagee to disclose:

(a) Property: property address, title number (if registered), and whether it is freehold or leasehold. In case of a leasehold property, obtain a copy of a lease (counterpart), the name and address of the landlords or their agents. Enquire if the landlords' consent to the charge is required. Is ground rent in arrears? By how much? Find out the amount of ground rent received, and the names of the parties to a lease.

Obtain a copy of the last assignment or conveyance in favour of the mortgagor to check the correct name in which it is assigned or conveyed (if unregistered).

(b) Mortgage: the original amount secured and the amount currently outstanding. If payments of capital and interest are up to date or if there are any arrears. Has notice of a further charge been received? If so, obtain name and address of the chargee.

(c) Insurance: name and address of the insurance company, policy number, and amount of the cover. Are premiums paid up to date?

(d) Consolidation: is the first mortgagee entitled to consolidate other debts?

(e) Further advances: is the first mortgagee under an obligation to make further advances? According to the Law of Property Act 1925, s.94(1), a prior mortgagee has a right to make further advances. The mortgage deed may impose an obligation to make further advances ('tacking'); or priority of further advances may have been agreed by the second mortgagee (usually by a 'deed of postponement'); or where first mortgagee has not received a notice of second mortgage when making further advances.

3. Consent of first mortgagee or lessor (additional procedure)
Before the mortgage is executed, obtain a written consent of the first mortgagee or lessor if required.

4. Land Charges searches and bankruptcy searches
Complete form K15 (it is important that the spelling of the chargors' names coincides with the deeds). This is to ensure that no other interest or charge is registered which will rank ahead of the first mortgage to be taken. If the reply is ' no subsisting entry', then it is safe to proceed.

5. Apply for a 'bankruptcy only' search on form K16.

6. Carry out local land charges search.

7. Obtain details of occupancy and waivers as already discussed under first mortgage of unregistered land.

8. *Execution of mortgage*

Proceed as already discussed under first mortgage procedure unregistered land. Additionally, the name of the first mortgagee and the date of their mortgage will be required to be inserted in the charge form.

9. *Valuation (amended procedure)*

Calculate the net amount of equity available between the value of the property and the amount outstanding with the first mortgagee. Ensure sufficient margin exists to cover the bank's lending. Lending value will be calculated by each institution in accordance with their formula.

10. *Insurance (amended procedure)*

(a) In the case of a freehold property, usually the first mortgagee will insure the property or see that the borrower has insured up to the reinstatement value advised by the valuer.

(b) If it is a leasehold property:
  (i)   the first mortgagee will ensure that insurance is arranged in accordance with the terms of the lease. Give notice to the insurance company, asking them to acknowledge the notice confirming the bank's interest in the policy and also confirming that premiums are up to date.
  (ii)   give notice to the lessor in duplicate (each lender has a standard form), requesting acknowledgement of the notice.

11. *Registration of the mortgage (amended procedure)*

(a) Register the legal mortgage in the Land Charges Register on form K1 as a puisne mortgage, i.e. class C(i), and as class C(iii) if it is a general equitable charge, so that the bank can have a priority over subsequent legal or equitable mortgagees.

(b) The Land Charges Registry will return the official search certificate quoting the reference number under which the application is registered.

(c) If the official search reply shows 'no subsisting entry', the bank will have a second charge.

(d) Upon receipt of the reply, make a further search on form K15 to check the bank's charge has been registered as a C(i) entry.

(e) If the property is charged by a limited company, register at Companies Registry within 21 days of execution of the charge.

12. Notice to the first mortgagee (additional procedure)
Give notice in duplicate (usually on the standard form of each bank) and ask first chargee to acknowledge and confirm the amount outstanding under their mortgage. Enquire if they have received notice of a subsequent charge, if payments are up to date, whether or not they intend to take action under their security, and if they are under an obligation to make any further advances.

By giving notice to the first mortgagee:

(a) the first mortgagee is prevented from making further advances which will have priority over the second mortgage to be taken (this is vital if the first mortgage has been given to secure a current account or other further advances), unless the first mortgagee has a right to 'tack' because of an obligation imposed in the mortgage deed to make further advances, or the second mortgagee consents to such further advances having priority.

(b) it imposes upon the mortgagee a duty to forward the deeds to the second mortgagee when the first mortgage is discharged. Registration without notice is not sufficient because the mortgagee is under no duty to search when the mortgage is discharged.

Section 95 of the Law of Property Act 1925 states that the mortgagee will not be regarded as having notice of a subsequent charge because it has been registered as a land charge, or in the local deeds registry, if it was not registered before the original advance was made or the last search was made.

(c) it will ensure that surplus proceeds, if any, are forwarded to the second mortgagee from the sale of the property.

5.8 EQUITABLE MORTGAGE

5.8.1 Specific considerations

Apart from the general considerations discussed earlier, the following should also be borne in mind.

If an equitable mortgage over unregistered land is given as security, do not accept only the deposit of title deeds, but also obtain a signed memorandum of deposit from the owner. According to s.2 of the Law of Property (Miscellaneous Provisions) Act 1989, any contract for future disposition of an interest in land is required to be in writing, signed by all parties, and it must include all the terms and conditions agreed by the parties.

Most lenders' memorandums of deposit contain some of the usual covenants and clauses found in the legal mortgage forms: i.e. continuing security clause; confirmation not to create any further charge without the bank's written consent; and to arrange insurance. If the mortgagor fails to insure, the bank can insure and charge the premiums to his account. This applies only to mortgages made by deed (Law of Property Act 1925 ss. 101 and 108) and restriction on consolidation and power to grant leases are excluded.

Section 2 of the Law of Property (Miscellaneous Provisions) Act 1989, which came into force on 27 September 1989 repealed s. 40 of the Law of Property Act 1925. Before this new provision came into force, equitable mortgages could be created by deposit of title deeds, which constituted a sufficient act or past performance to support the oral agreement, though they were usually taken with a signed and sealed memorandum incorporating the terms of the equitable charge. It was considered that by affixing a seal, the equitable mortgage would constitute a 'deed' and give the equitable mortgagee a power of sale (s.101 Law of Property Act 1925). Since s.1 of the Law of Property (Miscellaneous Provisions) Act 1989 states that a seal is no longer necessary for the valid execution of an instrument as a deed, lenders will have to consider this aspect when lending against the security of equitable mortgages supported by deposit of deeds, as they can no longer be regarded as effective.

Most memorandums of deposit also incorporate a clause whereby the customer undertakes to execute a legal mortgage when called upon to do so. They may also incorporate other covenants, remedies, powers and provisions, irrevocable power of attorney clause and/or a declaration of trust clause, as deemed fit by the lender's solicitors.

5.8.2   Joint tenancy in joint names

Where an equitable mortgage over property in joint names under joint tenancy is taken, obtain consent from both parties (husband and wife) to deposit title deeds or land certificate as security: *Thames Guaranty Ltd* v *Campbell & Others* [1984]. To be an effective equitable charge, the bank must be able to retain the title deeds until the debt has been repaid. The party whose consent is not taken is entitled at any time to a joint custody of the deeds, having joint title. He or she could request them to be returned, thus affecting the bank's security.

5.8.3 Equitable mortgage under hand/by deed

The advantage of an equitable mortgage executed by deed, as opposed to that under hand must be considered.

Some banks have a special type of equitable mortgage by deed.

According to s.101, of the Law of Property Act 1925, powers of sale and the power to appoint a receiver are available to those mortgagees whose mortgages are made by deed.

The equitable mortgagee has a statutory power to sell the property, but cannot convey the legal estate to the purchaser. Banks overcome this difficulty by incorporating in the deed an irrevocable power of attorney clause and a declaration of trust clause. This power cannot be revoked by the death, incapacity or bankruptcy of the donor; or, if the donor is a corporate body, then by dissolution or winding up (Powers of Attorney Act 1971, s.4(1)).

Equitable charge is only binding on those who are aware of it.

Building societies usually do not lend against security of an equitable charge.

5.8.4 Taking the security

The steps already explained for a first mortgage of unregistered land apply here and are only listed for reference purposes. However, slightly amended steps, as outlined below, will apply in respect of execution, insurance and leasehold property.

1. Investigate the title.
2. Value the security.
3. Search at the Land Charges Registry on form K15, and check that there are no prior charges or encumbrances registered affecting the security.
4. Search at the Local Land Charges Registry.
5. If a charge by a limited company is given, search at Companies Registry.
6. Apply for a 'bankruptcy search' on form K16 at Land Charges Registry.
7. Execution (amended procedure): obtain a signed memorandum of deposit from the mortgagor. The bank should join in to execute the form. If the property is in joint names, obtain consent from both owners to deposit title deeds. It may be completed under hand or by deed if stronger remedies are required.
8. Insurance (amended procedure): give notice of the bank's interest in the policy and retain an acknowledged copy.
9. Some banks also obtain a signed memorandum of occupancy from the owners to ascertain if any equitable or overriding interests exist. If they do, then the bank must obtain waivers from them, postponing their interests in favour of the bank.

10.   Leasehold property (amended procedure): give notice to the landlord of the bank's equitable interest in the property.

If the bank takes a charge without deposit of title deeds, register a C(iii) general equitable charge to obtain priority over subsequent mortgages.

If the bank feels that they may require the mortgagor to execute a legal mortgage at a later stage, follow the procedure for perfecting first legal mortgage with the exception of having the deed signed so that it can be converted into a legal mortgage later.

5.9   SUB-MORTGAGES

5.9.1   Specific considerations

A sub-mortgage is a 'mortgage of a mortgage', so that the original lender borrows by mortgaging his mortgagor's security.

The original lender (mortgagee) will become sub-mortgagor, the new lender the sub-mortgagee, and the original mortgage becomes the head mortgage (the security).

A sub-mortgage can be legal or equitable.

The lender with a security of a sub-mortgage can, irrespective of the value of the security, only recover monies from the mortgagor, because the reductions are made by periodic instalments. It is therefore difficult for a sub-mortgagee to maintain the security margin and the bank should write down the value of the security *pro tanto,* whenever the monies are paid by the original mortgagor.

It is important to check that all the appropriate steps for completion of securities are taken by the head mortgagee, and that the standing of the head mortgagee is undoubted.

If there is a defect in completing or registering the security by the head mortgagee, the sub-mortgagee bank will have a defective security.

If the head mortgage is equitable, any sub-mortgage will be equitable.

5.9.2   Legal or equitable sub-mortgage of unregistered land

Taking the security
Some of the procedures for taking a sub-mortgage are the same as those for a first mortgage of registered or unregistered land, and are therefore only summarised. A lender should also pay attention to the following matters.

1.   Obtain deposit of title deeds and the head-mortgage (if unregistered land) and land certificate (if registered land). Examine title deeds, the title of the head mortgagor and check that the mortgage given by the customer to the head-mortgagee is perfect. If it is a leasehold property, examine the lease to check

if consent of the landlord is required, or whether notice of the charge must be given.

2. Ascertain the outstanding debt owed to the head-mortgagee and value the property. Lend against a lower value of the amounts between the two.

3. Search at Land Charges Department against the name of head-mortgagor, customer, and sub-mortgagor.

4. Search in Local Land Charges Register.

5. Enquire concerning the occupancy and obtain waivers if applicable.

6. Execution of mortgage form: follow the same procedure as discussed for a first mortgage of unregistered land.

Most banks have a special form of sub-mortgage. The schedule should describe the mortgage granted to the sub-mortgagor and details of the property charged.

Ask the sub-mortgagor to execute the form. For a sub-mortgage of registered land insert the title number.

7. The title deeds, head-mortgage and executed sub-mortgage will create a first legal mortgage (unregistered land). Registration at the Land Charges Registry is not required for unregistered land. In case of registered land, have the sub-charge registered by lodging the charge certificate and certified copy of the sub-mortgage at the Land Registry. A note of the sub-charge is then entered. The Land Registry will issue a sub-charge certificate to the bank.

8. Insurance: give notice in duplicate to the insurance company and ask them to acknowledge notice.

Send notice to the head mortgagor in duplicate requesting acknowledgement of receipt and confirming the amount outstanding on his charge. Obtain an undertaking from the head mortgagor to make all future payments direct to the bank. As payments from the head mortgagor are received, write down the value of the security.

An equitable sub-mortgage for registered land can be created by giving notice in duplicate on form 85A to the Registrar who will enter it in its records.

Banks also ask the customer to execute a form of legal sub-mortgage so that it can be registered if need arises later.

5.10   FIRST LEGAL MORTGAGE OF REGISTERED FREEHOLD OR LEASEHOLD LAND

5.10.1   Specific considerations

Apart from the general considerations discussed earlier, the following specific considerations in respect of registered land should be borne in mind.

1. Investigate the title

Check the proprietorship register in the Land Certificate to see if the title is absolute, good leasehold, qualified or possessory. If it is a qualified title, then it may be subject to:

(a) encumbrances or other entries on the register.

(b) overriding interests (s.70 Land Registration Act 1925); e.g. equitable interest of wife in matrimonial home if she has contributed towards purchase. The owner will be bound by these rights even if they are non-registrable. Enquire from the owner details of occupation to check if they exist or not: *Hodgson* v *Marks* [1971].

(c) minor interests, protected by an entry on the register, e.g. restrictive covenants, a caution or inhibition.

2. Priorities

(a) For registered land, priorities of mortgages and interests depend upon the date of the entries recorded at the Land Registry and not upon the date of the mortgage, except where any minor or overriding interests of the *Boland* type occur (s.70 Land Registration Act).

(b) The proposed lender can obtain protection by applying for a search, which will provide 30 days priority within which to register the mortgage.

(c) If the bank intends to register a legal charge where a prior equitable charge is already in existence, the Land Registry will refuse a notice of legal charge from the subsequent mortgagee bank. The legal mortgagee will therefore not gain priority over an equitable mortgagee, although it will have stronger remedies.

Under s. 64 of the Land Registration Act 1925, any registration must be accompanied by the Land Certificate unless it is already in the custody of the Registrar. In these circumstances the subsequent mortgagee can:

(i) register a caution on form 63 supported by a statutory declaration. It will not have a legal charge, but the Land Registry will advise of any further dealings with the property.

(ii) ask the prior mortgagee to register a legal charge, to enable the subsequent mortgagee to register its charge.

(iii) pay off the equitable charge if the property has sufficient equity.

(d)   Where two properties are incorporated in one set of deeds, and the customer wants to retain the title deeds which the bank is taking as security, protect the bank's position by registering a C(i) or C(iii) charge as appropriate.

(e)   The Registrar is obliged to give notice of an attempt to put further entries recorded on the register.

In order to claim reimbursement from the Land Registry in respect of any loss due to failure by the Land Registry to advise of an entry, when an overdraft secured by a registered charge is transferred from one branch to another, the Land Registry must be informed. The exception to this rule is s. 5 of the Law of Property (Amendment) Act 1926.

5.10.2   Taking the security

Many procedures for perfecting a first legal mortgage are common for registered and unregistered land. Those procedures which have already been detailed in the steps for a first mortgage of unregistered land are only briefly listed here. Amended procedures, which apply in respect of title deeds, searches at the Land Registry instead of the Land Charges Registry, and registration are detailed below.

From 1 December 1990 all areas in England and Wales are subject to compulsory registration on sale of freehold land, or the grant of assignment of a lease over 21 years. Check the entries in the Land Certificate, which is an evidence of title to the registered land.

1.   Obtain the Land Certificate
A Land Certificate or a Charge Certificate consists of three registers:

(a)   The property register gives title number and a short description of the property, states if it is freehold or leasehold, quotes reference to the Land Registry General Map, and outlines any restrictive covenants.

(b)   The proprietorship register shows the 'class of title', i.e. absolute, good leasehold, possessory or qualified. It gives the name and address of the registered proprietor and the date the title was registered. It also shows notices, cautions, inhibitions and bankruptcy.

(c)   The charges register shows entries relating to mortgages which have been registered. It also shows that the Land Certificate has been deposited with the Registry. Minor interests, which have been registered, will also show here.

Check the Land Certificate:

(a)   If the title is possessory or qualified, examine the title prior to registration as if the land was unregistered, or obtain a report on title from the solicitors.

(b)   The other possible titles without a state guarantee are:
   (i)   possessory, which can be converted by a freeholder after 15 years into an absolute title and by a leaseholder after 10 years in possession into a good leasehold title;
   (ii) qualified (very rare);
   (iii) good leasehold title, where the leaseholder's title is good, but the freehold is not absolute (it can be converted after 10 years in possession by the leaseholder or his successors into an absolute title).

(c)   If the title is absolute, security of the Land Certificate is sufficient without the title deeds. If title deeds are given, check that no overriding interests exist, there are no other charges or encumbrances, and that the property offered as security is the same as that described in the Land Certificate.

If the lender is uncertain as to whether any freehold or leasehold or a rent charge is registered, or whether any priority notices or cautions against first registration have been recorded in the register, apply for an official search of the index map on form 96 addressed to the relevant District Land Registry. Quote the full description and address of the property, or enclose a copy of an extract from the Ordnance Survey map showing the extent of the property.

2.   *Value the security.*

3.   *Official search of the Register*
To check if any adverse entries exist in the register:

(a)   send the Land Certificate to the registry to be brought up to date;

(b)   make an official search on form 94A in duplicate (for a search of the whole of the land in the title) or form 94B in duplicate (for a search of part of the title) to the relevant District Land Registry with an appropriate fee. If a credit account facility is held with the Land Registry, then insert allocated key number.

The date entered on 94A or 94B for the commencement of the search should be either the date on which an office copy of the subsisting entries in the registry was issued, or the last date on which the land or charge certificate was compared with the land register.

If form 94B is sent, a copy of the filed plan marked in colour with the area to be searched must be attached.

The result of search will be sent on form 94D and will show any adverse entries, pending applications not yet entered on the register, and any other official search with unexpired priority affecting the land. It will show the expiry date and a priority period of 30 days will be given within which to register a charge.

If the lender wishes to ascertain whether any further entries have been recorded since the date of a recent office copy, form 94C search without priority can be sent, e.g. where the lender wants to protect his mortgage on the register by a notice of deposit of Land Certificate or a caution. The result of the search will not give priority for registration of any dealings.

4.   Bankruptcy only search
Apply for a bankruptcy search on form K16.

5.   Local land charges search
Carry out a local search at the appropriate local authority.

6.   Occupancy
Enquire the details of occupancy and obtain necessary waivers.

7.   Execution of the mortgage
The documents should be executed in accordance with the provisions of s. 2 Law of Property (Miscellaneous Provisions) Act 1989, and the problems arising as a result of a claim for undue influence and misrepresentation should be considered.

(a)   Prior to the execution of the mortgage, send the Land Certificate to the Land Registry to be brought up to date.

(b)   If only part of the title comprised in the land is charged, then a description by plan or reference to the Land Registry General Map is required. Arrange for the mortgage to be executed.

The execution of the mortgage must be by a deed and the mortgagee should

99

also join in the mortgage by having the mortgage signed by an authorised bank official. The name of the principal debtor or mortgagor, description of the property, title number and date of execution should be inserted. The signature of the mortgagor must be witnessed.

(c) If only part of the title comprised in the land is charged, then a description by plan or reference to the Land Registry General Map is required.

8. Registration
Send the mortgage to the Land Registry for registration, within the priority period or the extended priority period. Complete form A4 and send with it: the Land Certificate, executed legal mortgage (deed) and a certified copy, the official result of search 94A or 94B reply, a cheque representing payment of the scale fee and a certificate from the bank indicating the reliance placed on the security (i.e. lower value of the land or the facility given).

The table of fees for registration of charge is contained in Land Registration Fees (No. 2) Order.

For first registrations, or where a charge for transfer value is lodged, registration fee is not payable.

If the charge is executed by a limited company, then send it to the Companies Registry for registration within 21 days of execution.

The Land Registry will retain copy of the charge and the Land Certificate and issue the charge certificate.

Obligations to make further advances
Land Registration Rules 1925, Rule 139 and 139A (as amended by the Land Registration (Charges) Rules 1990)
For the purpose of the Land Registration Act 1925, s. 30(3), where a charge is already registered which contains an obligation to make further advances, the registration or renewal of registration of a notice or caution under the Act will be regarded as a subsequent registered charge which will take effect subject to any further advance made pursuant to that obligation. Accordingly, the statutory notice will be served by the Chief Land Registrar on the prior chargees in both these instances. But the Land Registry will not serve notice of the application upon the registered proprietor of the land.

Section 30(3) of the Land Registration Act 1925 provides, in effect, that if no note on the register is made, a subsequent registered charge takes effect free from any further advance made pursuant to an obligation. If a charge is altered to include an obligation under s. 31 (rule 150), the same principles apply.

In respect of any charge lodged for registration on or after 1 May 1991 (whether executed before that date or not), the Chief Land Registrar will not be under any duty to identify in the terms of the charge any obligation to make further advances. Instead, if the lender wishes s. 30(3) of the Land Registration Act 1925 to apply to the charge, either the instrument of charge itself must incorporate the modified new statutory application form 113, or a separate application in form 113 must be lodged.

No existing reference to an obligation, either in the instrument of charge or in any incorporated document, will be sufficient, in the absence of a specific application in accordance with the new rule.

Form 113
Rule 139A prescribes form 113 as the mandatory form for the application to note that an obligation is contained in a charge. The form is available from HMSO.

Rather than using a separate form 113, applicants may incorporate the operative parts of that form in an instrument of charge.

9. Insurance
Follow the procedure detailed in the first mortgage of unregistered land (freehold or leasehold).

10. If the land is leasehold follow the procedure detailed in the first mortgage of unregistered land (freehold or leasehold).

5.11 ANOTHER METHOD OF CREATING A MORTGAGE OF REGISTERED LAND

According to s.106 of the Land Registration Act 1925 (as amended by s. 26 of the Administration of Justice Act 1977), the owner of any registered land may mortgage by deed or otherwise the land or any part of it in any manner which would have been permissible if the land had not been registered.

Unless and until the mortgage becomes a registered charge, it takes effect only in equity. It can be overridden as a minor interest unless it is protected by a notice under s. 49, or by such other notice as may be prescribed or by caution under s. 54.

If the Land Certificate makes reference to restrictive covenants or to other interests affecting the title, a report on title from the solicitor may be obtained.

Fire insurance, local land charges searches, memorandum of occupancy and applicable waivers as discussed under unregistered (first mortgage) land will also apply here.

If the title is leasehold, obtain not only the Land Certificate, but also the head lease, together with any assignments that form a chain of title. Clauses and covenants of the lease should be examined, and other formalities for leasehold title as discussed under first mortgage unregistered land will apply.

5.12 SECOND MORTGAGE OF REGISTERED FREEHOLD OR LEASEHOLD LAND

5.12.1 Taking the security

A bank will only take a second mortgage over registered land by way of a legal mortgage so that it will have a registered charge.

Follow the same procedures as detailed for a second mortgage of unregistered land (freehold or leasehold), except for the following amended and additional procedures.

1. Prior mortgage enquiry
If the enquiry reveals consent from prior mortgagee is required, such a consent to register a second charge must be obtained.

Whilst making a prior mortgage enquiry from a first mortgagee, enquire if the first mortgagee has lent against the security of an endowment policy. If so, make a record of this. If the customer defaults and the second mortgagee has to realise its security, then a notice to the first mortgagee can be given to marshall its security under the equitable 'Doctrine of Marshalling' thereby requesting them to utilise the sums due under the policy first, in reduction of their debt. (This applies for registered and unregistered land.)

2. Official searches of office copies (additional procedure)
From 3 December 1990 the Land Registry is open to the public and any person, on payment of fees, may inspect and make copies of and extracts from entries on the register and documents mentioned therein.

(a)   Apply for official searches of office copies on form 109 (one form for each title) with appropriate fees, if a credit account is not held. If a credit account is held, then insert the key number to the relevant District Land Registry.

(b)   If the title number is not known, complete form 109 with the full address of the property.

(c)   If copies of personal covenants referred to in the register are required, then form 110 must be sent and form 110A, if office copy of a caution title is required.

(d)   Where only part of the land in the title is being charged, e.g. mostly in case of registered building developments where the Registry has approved an estate layout plan, make an application on form 109 for a certificate in form 102, with a copy of a plan (duplicate) and edging in colour the extent of the area covered, if the plot cannot be identified by the plot number(s) indicated on the approved layout plan. Appropriate fees must also be remitted.

Applications for office copies can be made by telephone or facsimile transmission at certain district Land Registries.

3. Valuation
Arrange for the valuation to be carried out. (See 5.5.3 and 5.6.1.)

4.   Official searches of the Register (amended procedure)
The second mortgagee will not have a security of a Land Certificate, as this will be held with the first mortgagee. Make an official search on form 94A in duplicate, as detailed in the procedure for first mortgage of registered land.

5.   In respect of a leasehold property, obtain the landlord's consent to charge, if the lease so requires.

6.   Apply for local land charges search.

7.   Enquire details of occupancy and obtain applicable waivers.

8.   Arrange for the mortgage to be executed.

9.   If the property is charged by a limited company, carry out a company search.

10.   Give notice to prior mortgagee or landlord.

11.   Give notice to insurance company, and ask them to acknowledge the notice confirming note of the bank's interest in the policy.

12.   Registration (amended procedure)
For registration at the Land Registry follow the same procedure as for registration of a first mortgage of registered land, but instead of forwarding a Land Certificate with A4 form, send office copy of the Land Certificate, and consent of the prior mortgagee in cases where restriction of a further charge without the first mortgagee's consent is registered at Land Registry.

The Land Registry will return second charge certificate which will show the first mortgagee's charge and the bank's second charge in the charges register.

If the first mortgagee has not registered its charge, but only a notice of deposit, then the second mortgagee bank's interest can be protected by registering a caution. The second mortgagee bank may request the first chargee bank to register its charge and then perfect (register) a second charge in the usual way.

To ensure that in between the time when the prior mortgage enquiry was made in respect of the amount outstanding with the first mortgagee and the time when monies are advanced after completion of registration formalities, the borrower has not borrowed further monies against the same mortgage from the prior mortgagee, obtain details of the current outstanding amount from the first mortgagee before advancing the monies.

5.13 EQUITABLE MORTGAGE OF REGISTERED FREEHOLD OR LEASEHOLD LAND

An equitable mortgage of registered land can be obtained by following alternative procedures depending on the circumstances.

5.13.1 Notice of deposit

1. Send form 85A in duplicate signed by the manager or authorised official, together with the Land Certificate to the Land Registry for registering a notice of deposit.

2. If the customer does not wish an entry of notice of deposit recorded on the Land Certificate, then send the Land Certificate first to be brought up to date. When it is returned, send form 85A/85B in duplicate without the Land Certificate for the notice to be registered.

3. The Land Registry will return one copy of form 85A (duly stamped) with an entry in the Land Certificate entered.

4. Registration of entry of notice of deposit will protect the bank against subsequent encumbrance. If the owner attempts to make any disposition of land, the Land Registry will advise the equitable mortgagee and give him 14 days to protect his position, i.e. to register a legal mortgage.

5.13.2 Notice of deposit and legal mortgage held unregistered

1. The bank may adopt one of the following procedures.

    (i)   Although notice of deposit of a Land Certificate recorded at the Land Registry is sufficient to create an equitable charge, some banks use a memorandum of deposit under hand for this purpose.

This will not give the bank power to sell the property if the mortgagor defaults; or,

(ii) obtain from the mortgagor an equitable mortgage by deed, which contains the usual clauses, which will confer power upon the bank to sell if the mortgagor defaults; or,

(iii) obtain from the mortgagor an executed legal mortgage and hold it unregistered. Give notice of deposit on duplicate form 85A to the Land Registry.

2. If the mortgagor defaults and the bank wishes to enforce its security, or if Land Registry advise subsequent dealings, register the charge at the Land Registry. In *Barclays Bank Ltd* v *Taylor* [1973], this procedure was held to be effective.

Section 26 of the Administration of Justice Act 1977 removes any doubt concerning the practice in that notice of deposit given in accordance with Rule 239 of the Land Registry Rules 1925 operates as a caution under s. 54 of the Land Registration Act 1925.

5.13.3 Notice of intended deposit

1. If there is an intention to create an equitable or legal mortgage, but if the Land Certificate is not available, because the borrower who has agreed to purchase the property will not be able to produce the Land Certificate until it has been issued to him, then:

(a) lodge Notice of Deposit on form 85B (in duplicate) to the Land Registry (if the land is being registered for the first time); or,

(b) use form 85C (if the title is already registered, but when there is an incomplete dealing with registered land).

2. The Land Registry will return the Land Certificate to the mortgagee bank or its solicitor.

5.13.4 Taking the security

This procedure is usually followed when the method described in 5.13.2 is used.
1. Obtain the Land Certificate.
2. Value the security.
3. Search at the Local Land Charges registry.
4. To ascertain that there are no adverse entries in the register, send the Land Certificate to the registry with form 85A/85B (as applicable) in duplicate.

The Land Registry will bring the Land Certificate up to date and record a notice of deposit.

When the Land Certificate is received back from the Land Registry, check there are no adverse entries affecting the security.

5.   If the customer does not wish the entry of the notice of deposit recorded on the Land Certificate, then send the Land Certificate first to be brought up to date. When it is returned, send form 85A/85B in duplicate, without the Land Certificate, for the notice to be registered or make a personal search and, if clear, lodge a notice of deposit.

6.   Obtain a signed memorandum of deposit under hand or by deed or an executed legal mortgage if the bank wants to hold a legal mortgage unregistered.

7.   Obtain details of occupancy or applicable waivers if the method in 5.13.2 is used. Most banks follow this procedure, although the mere deposit of a Land Certificate, followed by the lodging of notice on forms 85A/85B, is sufficient to create an equitable mortgage.

In respect of the procedure for insurance and for leasehold properties, follow the procedure discussed for a first mortgage of unregistered land.

5.14   DISCHARGE OF MORTGAGES OR RELEASE OF SECURITY

(as regards registered and unregistered land)

5.14.1   First mortgage of unregistered land

Two methods available for discharge of a legal mortgage are:

1.   (a)   A statutory form of receipt, usually with standard wordings, printed on or endorsed on most banks' mortgage forms, should be signed by the mortgagee bank under hand or seal depending on the bank's own rules. The same wordings may be used for both freehold or leasehold land.

The receipt confirms acknowledgement of the monies received and the name of the person who pays the money must be stated.

(b)   Hand the vacated mortgage, which forms a link in the title, with an endorsed receipt on to the customer, together with the title deeds against his/her receipt.

(c)   If the bank has received a notice of a second mortgage, then do not pass on the vacated mortgage and title deeds to the customer, but send them to the second mortgagee.

(d)   Advise the insurance company, informing them that the bank no longer has an interest in the fire insurance policy.

(e)   If a third party has paid the money, unless otherwise expressly stated, it operates 'as if the benefit of the mortgage had by deed been transferred to him'; e.g. where a guarantor pays off the whole debt in respect of security deposited to secure the customer's borrowing, the guarantor is entitled to have those securities transferred to him.

2.   Alternatively the bank can transfer the mortgage to the guarantor/third party by way of a separate deed.

If the bank as a first mortgagee has exercised its power of sale, and after discharging its mortgage debt has a surplus, search the Land Charges Register. The bank would be liable to any subsequent registered mortgagee if it paid the surplus to the customer.

If the whole debt secured by the mortgage is not being repaid, or where only a part of the land in the title is being released from the charge, a bank may discharge a mortgage by an endorsement on the mortgage made under seal, or as a reconveyance of the property to the mortgagor, or by a separate deed of release.

5.14.2   Equitable mortgage of unregistered land

1.   A bank can discharge an equitable mortgage by a separate form of a simple receipt, or by writing 'cancelled' across the memorandum of deposit and handing back the deeds to the customer against receipt.

The method of discharge varies from one bank to another and a formal surrender or statutory receipt is not necessary.

2.   If the mortgage has been taken without the deposit of title deeds, the bank would have registered a C(iii) (general equitable charge) and should arrange to have this charge deleted in the Land Charges Register by forwarding form K11.

3.   Give notice of bank's release to the first mortgagee and insurance company.

5.14.3   Second mortgage of unregistered land

1.   The bank as second mortgagee will have a legal mortgage without deposit of title deeds, i.e. a puisne mortgage, which the bank would have registered as a C(i) charge.

2.   Send form K11 duly signed by an authorised official to the Land Charges Registry for the entry to be deleted from their records.

3.   Send the vacated bank mortgage, which forms a part of the chain of title, to the first mortgagee to retain it with the deeds, and ask them to acknowledge receipt.

4.   Give notice of release of bank's second charge to the first mortgagee and, if appropriate, to the insurance company.

5.14.4   Sub-mortgage

If a legal sub-mortgage is to be discharged, endorse on the sub-mortgage a receipt. Each bank usually has a standard wording for this receipt.

5.14.5   Release of part security

1.   A legal mortgage cannot be discharged by endorsing a partial receipt on the deed.

2.   Complete a separate deed of discharge, clearly showing the extent of the land released.

3.   If it is an equitable mortgage, give a simple receipt to the borrower (each bank will have standard wordings for the receipt).

5.14.6   First legal mortgage of registered land

The following changes were introduced on 1 May 1991 by the Land Registration (Charges) Rules 1990:

Section 26 Land Registration Rules 1925 as amended by the Land Registration (Charges) Rules 1990

New Rule 151 (Part IV)

Discharge of a registered charge

1.   A discharge wholly or in part of a registered charge shall be made by an instrument in form 53 and shall:

(a)   in the case of an individual, be signed by the proprietor of the charge;

(b)   in the case of a proprietor of a charge being a company registered under the Companies Acts be executed:

(i)   under seal in accordance with s. 74(1) of the Law of Property Act 1925; or

(ii)   in accordance with s. 36A of the Companies Act 1985; or

(iii)   otherwise in such manner as the Registrar is satisfied may be authorised under its articles of association;

(c) in the case of any other corporate body either:
  (i) be executed under seal in accordance with s. 74(1) of the Law of Property Act 1925; or
  (ii) be signed or executed by such person as the Registrar is satisfied has authority, under the instrument or statute constituting or regulating the affairs of the proprietor or otherwise, to bind the proprietor in the discharge of the charge;
but the Registrar shall be at liberty to accept and act upon any other proof of satisfaction of a charge which he may deem sufficient.

2. (a) Complete LR form 53 and send it to the relevant district Land Registry with the charge certificate. The form should be signed by the authorised signatory of the bank. This form need not be sealed; or

(b) Complete a copy of the bank's own form 53, where the Land Registry has approved this form of discharge, and send duly signed or sealed form to the relevant District Land Registry. No fee is payable for the discharge.

3. If part only of the land is being released, the following words should be added on the form: 'As to the land shown and edged with red on the accompanying plan, signed by me, being part of the land comprised in the said charge'. In this case attach with form 53 a general map, the Ordnance Map or the filed plan clearly showing the extent of area being released (edged in red).
  If the mortgagor has sold the property then complete form 55 which is a combined form of transfer and discharge. The form should be executed by the mortgagor and mortgagee of the charge.

Discharge of legal charge by building societies
Building societies can discharge their legal mortgages in the following ways:

Unregistered land
1. In accordance with Schedule 4, paragraph 2 of the Building Societies Act 1986, most legal charges will have a printed form of receipt on the back.
  Arrange for the receipt to be sealed and countersigned by a person authorised by the board of directors. This receipt does not require the name of the person redeeming the loan to be inserted and is therefore preferred by building societies.
  Follow the actual wordings provided in a statutory instrument, The Building Societies (Supplementary Provisions as to Mortgages) Rules 1986; or
2. Use a form of statutory receipt (all lenders may use this) provided by Schedule 3 of the Law of Property Act 1925. The lenders may vary this and

one receipt will discharge all mortgages advanced against the security of the property.

It is not necessary to execute this receipt under seal, but in practice most lenders do so.

3.   Instead of using a statutory receipt, re-convey the property to the borrower or to a person nominated by the borrower.

Registered land

Building societies use form 53, as used by all lenders to discharge a mortgage over registered land. Form 53 must be sealed and countersigned by a person authorised by the board of directors.

After discharge

1.   If no other charge is registered, the Land Registry will delete the bank's charge from the register, bring the Land Certificate up to date and return it to the bank.

2.   Return the Land Certificate to the registered proprietor against his receipt.

5.14.7   Second mortgage of registered land

Follow the same procedure as that of a release of a first mortgage of registered land, but instead of a first charge certificate, send a second charge certificate and form 53 to the relevant District Land Registry.

As the charge in favour of the first mortgagee will still be outstanding, the Land Registry will not release the Land Certificate, but will acknowledge that it has deleted the record of the second charge from the register.

5.14.8   Equitable mortgage of registered land

1.   If the bank has taken an equitable mortgage only by forwarding forms 85A/85B or 85C as appropriate without sending the Land Certificate, then complete (the duplicate of these forms) the withdrawal form 86, which constitutes an addition to these original forms. Form 86 should be duly signed by an authorised official of the bank and sent to the relevant District Land Registry.

2.   If the Land Certificate was also sent with these forms to the Land Registry when an equitable charge was registered, send the Land Certificate with the withdrawal form 86 for the entry therein to be deleted.

3.   The Land Registry will delete the entry of the notice of deposit from its register, and from the Land Certificate, and return the Land Certificate to the bank.

4.   Hand the Land Certificate to the customer against receipt.

5. If the bank has obtained a legal mortgage, or a memorandum of deposit, or a form of equitable charge, then mark 'cancelled' on the form and retain it with the security. Some solicitors may request a release executed on the mortgage.

6. Where part of the land in the title is charged, then unless that part is being sold, it is not possible to withdraw notice of deposit.

7. Upon sale of that part, the bank mortgagee may give its consent to dealing with part of the land, and advise the Registrar whether it requires the dealing to be registered free from this lien.

8. If it is on unregistered land, withdrawal of notice of the bank's interest must be given to the insurance company.

9. If the lender is a second mortgagee, give notice of release to the first mortgagee.

10. Where a bank holds, as security, an unregistered legal mortgage duly protected by a caution, then apply for withdrawal of the caution from the proprietorship register on form 71, which is required to be executed by the bank or its solicitors.

5.14.9   Matrimonial

1. Where a wife's rights of occupation have been brought to an end, in case of unregistered land, a Class F entry in the Land Charges Register can be cancelled by completing and forwarding form K13.

2. In case of registered land, send a simple letter or form 202 with the necessary evidence to the relevant District Land Registry.

3. If a caution is registered, send a simple letter or send completed form 71 duly signed by the wife or her solicitors.

5.14.10   Release of deeds or Land Certificate for inspection and return

If the deeds have to be released to the customer's solicitors when drainage rights or obligations in respect of boundary fences have to be checked:

(a)   obtain customer's written instructions for this purpose;

(b)   list the deeds and schedule them, either on a separate form or on the undertaking form and ask the solicitors to acknowledge receipt. Do not send the bank mortgage form (for unregistered land).

Some banks retain the last conveyance and send only a copy of it to the solicitors.

5.14.11 Release of deeds or Land Certificate upon sale or re-mortgage

1.   Obtain the customer's written authority to forward deeds, the Land Certificate or charge certificate to the customer's solicitors.

2.   Obtain a bank reference on the solicitors, if the bank has not had dealings with them in the past.

3.   If repayment to the bank is to be made from the re-mortgage, enquire the amount which the new lender has agreed to lend, supported by proof of an accepted mortgage offer.

4.   If the property is being sold, enquire the sale price, whether contracts are exchanged or not, and the completion date.

5.   If contracts have not been exchanged, send the deeds (if unregistered) with the schedule (listing them in the date order), or copies of entries from the Land Certificate or charge certificate, with details of the last date compared. Also send a certified copy of lease (if leasehold), with the bank's standard form of undertaking for inspection and return.

If contracts have been exchanged, an appropriate undertaking must be obtained from the solicitor. Usually the banks' standard forms contain wordings for this purpose, to the effect that they will hold the deeds to the bank's order until completion; and on completion forward net sale proceeds of not less than a stated amount, after deducting estate agent's costs, fees and disbursements; and to return them to the bank on demand in the same condition if the sale does not proceed.

6.   Once net proceeds of the sale are received, vacate the legal mortgage (if unregistered) or issue form 53 (if registered) or form 86 (if notice of deposit), and send it to the solicitor.

5.15   MONITORING

5.15.1   Matrimonial

1.   If a mortgagee intends to bring an action against a spouse who has protected his or her rights of occupation (of a dwelling house) by registering a Class F charge (unregistered land) at Land Charges Registry or by a notice of caution (registered land), serve notice of the action on the spouse (s. 8(3) of the Matrimonial Homes Act 1983).

2.   To ascertain (in the case of registered land) if a notice or a caution to protect a spouse's rights of occupation has been registered, apply for an official certificate of the result of a search by forwarding form 106 in duplicate to the relevant District Land Registry. No fee is payable.

If the land is unregistered, carry out a search on form K15.

5.15.2 Granting subsequent leases

A mortgagor, who has mortgaged property to the bank and subsequently intends to rent the property, must obtain prior written consent of the bank, otherwise the tenancy will be void: *Dudley and District Building Society* v *Emerson* [1949].

If the mortgagor has rented the property without obtaining the bank's permission, and if the bank later becomes aware of such a tenancy, the bank must take action immediately to protect its interest. Otherwise it will be stopped from denying that it had accepted the situation, e.g. where the bank opens a new account for the mortgagor and collects rental income.

5.15.3 Notice of subsequent charge

1. If a notice of subsequent charge is received, acknowledge the notice.
2. Mark the bank's records with details of the subsequent mortgage. After the receipt of a subsequent mortgage, a bank cannot make further advances to rank in priority to the subsequent charge without the subsequent mortgagee's consent. If the bank's mortgage form imposes an obligation on the bank to make further advances, this position is of course covered.
3. The action to be taken will depend on whether it is a loan account or an overdrawn account.

Loan account

1. If a borrower has a loan account and also a credit balance on the current account, after receipt of notice of a subsequent mortgage, combine both the accounts. If any cheques are received thereafter, the bank may dishonour them.
2. After receipt of a notice of a subsequent mortgage, it is not necessary for the bank to rule off the current account because the bank would have advised the amount of its priority, accrued interest and the amount of interest that will accrue in the future, when it would have acknowledged the notice of subsequent charge and therefore retained its priority up to the amount advised. But in practice most banks rule off the current account and open a new account after receipt of notice of a subsequent charge.
3. If it is a troublesome account, or where the bank anticipates that litigation is imminent, debit loan interest to the loan account to gain priority, so that it is not regarded as a new borrowing.

Current account

1. Upon request of a notice of a subsequent charge, 'rule off' the account to prevent the rule in *Clayton's* case from operating. Otherwise the first

mortgagee's priority will be reduced by payments into the account and subsequent withdrawals will rank behind that of the subsequent mortgagee.

Failure to do so can result in possible postponement of the full amount secured under the first mortgage. This will rank behind the subsequent mortgage, which will gain priority over it: *Deeley* v *Lloyds Bank Ltd* [1912].

2.   Open a new current account and credit all future transactions to this account, which should be operated in credit.

3.   Stop the account if notice of a Class F charge under Matrimonial Homes Act is received otherwise the lender's charge will rank behind that of the holder of a Class F charge.

4.   Where a lender has agreed an overdraft facility for a customer, upon receipt of notice of a subsequent charge, 'rule off' the account even if the overdraft limit has not been fully utilised.

A first mortgagee cannot prevent subsequent mortgages effected by registered disposition by merely incorporating a restriction in its mortgage form (Land Registration Act 1925, s. 25(3)), unless its restriction is protected by registering a caution on the register. In this case the Land Registry will advise the mortgagee of an attempt by a subsequent mortgagee to register a second mortgage.

5.   If a subsequent mortgagee has not registered its charge at the Land Charges Registry or at the Local Land Registry before the original advance was made, or the last search carried out by the prior mortgagee, the prior mortgagee will not be regarded as having received notice of this subsequent charge (s. 95 of The Law of Property Act 1925).

5.15.4   Further advances (building societies)

1.   For further advances made by building societies, normally a higher interest rate will be charged. The mortgagor will not qualify for MIRAS, and the amount of further advance will have gross interest charged.

2.   Whether a valuation for further advances will be required or not will depend on each lender's policy. Most lenders will insist on valuation before making further advances. Building society valuations for further advances are necessary where:

(a)   no prior valuations were carried out within previous two years;

(b)   property has been modified or structurally amended; or

(c)   further advance is for the purchase of additional land.

The borrower's position will be assessed, i.e. if there has been any material change in his employment, in which case a reference from his employer should be obtained.

3. If a guarantee is taken as security for a loan, obtain the guarantor's consent before making further advances.

4. Re-check the occupancy by obtaining details of the occupants. Obtain waivers from occupants who have not already executed waivers, postponing their rights to rank after the mortgagee's rights.

5. If further advances are made for the extension of the property, check that necessary planning approvals are held by the borrower.

5.15.5   Death of the borrower

1. If the sole borrower, who is the registered proprietor of the property, dies, the property will be vested in the administrators or executors of his estate.

2. Obtain the death certificate and in due course probate or letters of administration.

3. Payments due under the mortgage will usually be made by the personal representatives.

If payments are not made, consider taking legal action against the personal representatives for possession of the property.

4. Repayment, in most cases, will be made by the personal representatives from the sale of the property, or from the proceeds of an endowment policy if it is assigned to the bank.

5.15.6   Death of a person who is one of two or more joint borrowers as joint tenants

1. The mortgage and the property will be vested in the survivor(s).

2. In these circumstances, payments of the mortgage will be made by the surviving mortgagor(s).

3. Obtain the death certificate. The bank can either forward it with the charge certificate to the Land Registry, so that the deceased mortgagor's name is deleted from the records, or retain a certified copy of the death certificate and produce it with the charge certificate and form 53 when the property is sold.

5.15.7   Bankruptcy of the borrower

1. Write to the official receiver informing him of the amount of the outstanding debt, including interest, as at the date of the bankruptcy order. If it is a secured debt, details of the security charged and any other assets of the bankrupt that the bank may be aware of should be advised.

2.   If the bankrupt has signed a legal mortgage:

(a)   Give notice, calling up the security, to the mortgagor(s) and the trustee.

(b)   Check if any prior mortgagees propose to take any action. If not, as subsequent mortgagee, consider enforcement proceedings.

(c)   If sale of the property is to be effected, ask the trustee if he or she would be prepared to undertake the sale.

5.15.8   Equitable mortgages

Check with the trustee in bankruptcy if he will be prepared to act in realisation, otherwise obtain an order for sale from the court.

5.16   CLAUSES IN THE BANKS' MORTGAGE FORMS

The types of clauses which are invariably found in all bank mortgage forms, whatever the nature of the security, have already been discussed in Chapter 1. These clauses will also be found in the banks' standard legal or equitable mortgage forms, for the purpose of taking a charge over land. Additionally, the following specific clauses relating to a mortgage over land will be found in the mortgage forms.

1.   Personal covenant by the mortgagor to repay all sums due
This clause is found in most bank mortgage forms. Because of this clause, the bank must make demand on the mortgagor before it can sue so that the Limitation Act 1980 does not begin to operate against the bank until it makes a demand.

If this clause was not inserted, the time may run against the bank from the date of each advance.

Building society mortgage forms usually incorporate a clause which provides for regular repayment of capital and interest, if the loan is on an endowment basis, and that the lender will accept interest only on the payment as long as an endowment policy is assigned to it.

Because the covenant to repay is a personal covenant, the mortgagee could still have recourse against the mortgagor, even if the mortgagee has no charge over the property (i.e. it has sold the property for a lesser amount than the outstanding debt). In *West Bromwich Building Society* v *Bullock* [1936], the mortgagor was asked to make good the loss suffered by the building society after the sale.

2.   Covenants to repair and insure
The mortgagor covenants with the bank:

(a)   to keep the mortgaged property, fixtures, and machinery forming part of the premises, in a good state of repair and to insure them against loss or damage by fire to the full value of the property;

(b)   to effect insurance with a reputable insurance company acceptable to the bank, and on demand produce to the bank the policy and premium receipts;

(c)   if the mortgagor fails to keep buildings, fixtures and machinery in good repair, the bank is empowered to carry out the necessary repairs and to recover the costs from the mortgagor.

Most building societies have 'block' insurance schemes. In accordance with the 1978 agreement between the Office of Fair Trading and the Building Societies Association:

(a)   the borrower is given a choice of at least three insurance companies or allowed to arrange his own cover provided its terms meet the society's conditions and the cover meets the society's own block policy arrangements;

(b)   the borrower, by express clause in the legal charge, agrees to act as trustee of sums received under a claim and only apply them in accordance with the society's direction. This clause came into force following the decision in *Halifax Building Society* v *Keighley* [1931]. However, in case of leasehold property, insurance should be arranged in accordance with the terms and conditions of the lease.

If the mortgagor fails to insure against fire, to overcome the limited power of insurance conferred by the Law of Property Act 1925, ss. 101 and 108, some bank forms incorporate an express power to insure the property 'in such sums as the bank shall deem fit'.

Any monies received under an insurance policy, whether effected by the mortgagor or by the bank as mortgagee, are to be applied by the mortgagor if the mortgagee so requires, in making good the loss or damage, or to be utilised in reduction of the debt secured by the mortgage.

3.   Money due on demand
According to the Law of Property Act 1925, s.101, power of sale and power to appoint a receiver arise when the mortgage money has become due, i.e. when the mortgagor defaults after demand for repayment has been made. Most mortgage deeds usually state that money is due on demand.

As building society mortgages are not repayable on demand, but are usually for a fixed term, and the mortgagor covenants to repay fixed instalments, action under the building society mortgage can only be taken when the customer defaults in paying the instalment.

4. Power of sale and power to appoint a receiver

Most bank mortgage forms for this purpose exclude ss.103 and 109(1) of the Law of Property Act 1925, which requires at least three months' notice before exercising the power of sale and the power to appoint a receiver. Some banks' forms include a period of, say one month, while others state that the power can be exercised at any time after demand for repayment has been made on the mortgagor and the mortgagor has defaulted.

5. Consolidation clause

Power of consolidation by mortgagees was abolished by the Conveyancing Act 1881, which was re-enacted in s. 93 of the Law of Property Act 1925. According to s. 93 a mortgagor can redeem one mortgage without paying monies due under any separate mortgage given by him.

To overcome this problem bank mortgage forms include a clause which excludes the mortgagor's statutory right under s. 93, although a clause to this effect is not strictly necessary because all bank mortgage forms have an 'all monies due and owing on accounts …' clause.

6. Agreement not to create or surrender leases

To ensure that the value of the banks' security is not affected by unauthorised occupancy or tenancy, banks must ensure they can obtain vacant possession of the property for selling.

Section 99 of the Law of Property Act provides that a mortgagor has a power to grant agricultural or occupational leases, subject to certain conditions, for any term not exceeding 50 years and building leases not exceeding 999 years. The mortgagor in possession may accept surrender of any lease. The purpose of doing so is to grant a new lease, which falls within his statutory powers under s.100(1) of the Act.

To protect its position as mortgagee, bank mortgage forms exclude s. 99 and s.100 of the Law of Property Act 1925, restricting the mortgagor's power to grant leases without the bank's prior written consent. The only exception to this is that under the Agricultural Holdings Act 1948, a bank cannot exclude the statutory power of a mortgagor who is in possession to grant a lease of agricultural land. The lease would therefore be binding on the mortgagee bank: *Dudley & District Benefit Building Society* v *Emerson* [1949]; *Lloyds Bank Ltd* v *Marcan* [1973].

Mortgagees should not collect rent from a tenant and utilise it for reduction of the mortgage debt, as this will amount to a recognised tenancy. Where a tenancy existed prior to a lender taking the mortgage, it will be binding on the lender. If it is created after the mortgage is executed, unless express or implied consent is obtained, the lender will not be bound by it: *Dudley & District Benefit Building Society* v *Emerson* [1949]. Although the bank's mortgage forms restrict the mortgagor to grant leases without the bank's consent, banks may be subject to other risks which cannot be protected by any form of clauses or words in the mortgage. This was illustrated by the decisions in *Universal Permanent Building Society* v *Cooke* [1951]; and *Abbey National Building Society* v *Cann* [1990].

7. Attornment clause

Because the Rules of the Supreme Court as amended have made the speedy procedure of Order 14 available to mortgagees, banks no longer need to insert this clause. Some banks still incorporate it because by virtue of this clause, a mortgagee can obtain from Justices a warrant for possession under the Small Tenements Recovery Act 1938, s.1.

By a declaration of trust clause, the mortgagor confirms that he holds the property in a trust for the bank, and gives the bank a power to change trustees if it wishes, thus empowering the bank to appoint another person in place of the mortgagor.

8. Agreement to keep the covenants

In case of leasehold land, the mortgagor undertakes to comply with all the terms and conditions of the lease. These covenants are also included in the lease. Therefore there is no real need to include this clause in the mortgage, but some banks still do so.

9. The bank's consent is required before creating a further mortgage

Only some banks' forms incorporate this clause, to keep tighter control over their security and to afford a means whereby it is kept advised of attempts of subsequent dealings in land. Failure to comply with this clause will not render the subsequent mortgage void because this agreement is only between the bank and the mortgagor. If a subsequent mortgagee creates a mortgage when the prior mortgagee's mortgage form incorporates a restriction to create subsequent change, the first mortgagee will not acknowledge the bank's subsequent charge if the subsequent mortgagee had not sought its consent.

10.   Use of the property does not conflict with the Town and Country Planning Acts

The mortgagor covenants that the present use of the property conforms with the Town and Country Planning Acts. The mortgagor will not breach any conditions, erect additional buildings, make structural alterations or any material change in the use of the property without obtaining prior permission of the mortgagee and from the Planning Authority under the Act.

The mortgagor also confirms that he will allow the lender access for inspection, indemnify him against all actions, damages, costs, claims, acts, or omissions arising as required by the Act, and that upon default, the lender can arrange repair to be carried out and debit his account.

11.   'All monies' clause

This clause covers all liabilities of the mortgagor including interest and other costs incurred in enforcing the bank's security and contingent liabilities. Even if the principal debt is repaid and the latter costs remain, the bank is entitled to retain the security; for example, in the case of a company, until the risk of crystallisation has passed: *Re Rudd & Son Ltd* [1984].

5.16.1   Specific clauses contained in building society mortgage forms

In addition to some of the standard clauses contained in the legal charge forms mentioned above, the following specific clauses are also incorporated in building society mortgage forms.

(a)   Covenant to repay.

(b)   Interest clause.

   (i)   Building society forms have an additional clause whereby they have a right to vary the rate of interest (if not fixed rate mortgage), provided notice is given in accordance with the period and method as stated in the mortgage deed.

   (ii)   Charge compounding rate of interest on unpaid interest added to the mortgage debt, where repayments made are for a lesser sum than the interest being charged. However, following the decision in *Eastern Counties Building Society* v *Russell* [1947], a legal charge must allow such a right. A building society can make an index linked mortgage: *Nationwide Building Society* v *Registry of Friendly Societies* [1983].

(c)   Transfer of a mortgage – This clause allows the lender to transfer the loan to a third party subject to the same terms and conditions as the original charge. This power is hardly used. The clause also provides that the contract will continue if societies merge through an amalgamation or transfer of engagements.

In *Sun Permanent Benefit Building Society* v *Western Suburban and Harrow Road Permanent Building Society* [1921], it was held that to effect such a transfer, the building society's legal charge should incorporate power to do so, set out circumstances under which a transfer is possible and the benefits in respect of the payment of the capital and interest which are to pass on a transfer. All borrowings members' resolutions are required, where a merger is proposed and a mortgage is to be transferred because of an amalgamation (The Building Societies Act 1986, s.93(2) and (5)).

(d)   Partial repayment of capital – A building society's legal charge form of rules outlines the procedure for permitting borrowers to effect partial repayment of the capital over and above the normal repayments. This will usually apply in cases where the account is on a repayment basis.

(e)   Rules of membership – The legal charge includes a clause that a borrower acknowledges receipt of a copy of the rules of the society. The borrower confirms that, as a member of the society, he or she will be bound by the rules.

(f)   Guarantor or surety – Some building society legal mortgage forms have a provision for the name of the guarantor (if stipulated in the offer for advance) to be inserted. The guarantor is liable in cases where the principal debtor fails to comply with his obligations. The name of a surety, who will be required to guarantee repayment of capital plus interest if the mortgagor fails to carry out his obligations on the mortgage, is also provided.

(g)   Deduction of tax – This clause allows building societies to deduct the tax, where applicable in accordance with the conditions specified in the form.

(h)   Indemnity clause – A condition is provided giving the society powers to arrange indemnity policy (only if stipulated in the offer of advance), and to charge a single premium to the mortgagor unless otherwise agreed.

(i)   Income tax relief on house purchase – The mortgagor undertakes to complete the Inland Revenue MIRAS 70 form(s) and return it with the accepted offer.

(j)   Right to withdraw the offer – The building society has the right to withdraw the offer, notwithstanding previous acceptance, it may also vary its terms before the mortgage is entered into.

(k)   Retention from the loan – By this clause building societies have a right to release or retain any sum in accordance with the terms of the offer of advance.

5.17   REMEDIES OF A LEGAL MORTGAGEE

If the customer defaults and cannot discharge his debt, the lender, subject to the terms of the mortgage deed and the relevant sections of the Consumer Credit Act 1974, where appropriate, will have the following remedies, outlined in the Law of Property Act 1925. The remedies available will depend on whether mortgage is legal or equitable.

The lender can use any or all of the remedies outlined below, although in practice the lender usually obtains possession of the property and sells as mortgagee in possession.

1.   *Sue on the personal covenants*
This remedy is available even if no security is held. A lender may sue the borrower on his or her personal covenant for either the arrears or the total debt. This will only prove worthwhile if the debtor or mortgagor has funds, and pressure is necessary for repayment of the debt.

The lender will pursue this remedy only where:

(a)   the borrower needs to be sued in respect of the loss suffered by the lender from the sale of the property;

(b)   the account is in arrears, and the borrower has stopped making payments, then the lender (especially a building society) may decide to sue on the arrears.

If the lender has reason to believe that the borrower has the ability to repay but is avoiding his liability, a threat of bankruptcy proceedings may prove to be simpler and more effective than to realise the security. However, this course of action should be followed with caution.

2.   *Appoint a receiver*
Under s.101 and s.109 of the Law of Property Act 1925, a mortgagee has power to appoint a receiver, which is exercisable under the same conditions as power of sale. The appointment must be in writing under hand (s. 109(1)) and stamped.

The appointment is considered necessary in cases where property is tenanted or where the lender's security is a block of flats or business property, as it will not be easy to obtain vacant possession due to security of tenure.

Where large properties are included, it is advisable to appoint a professional estate agent or accountant as a receiver.

The receiver will apply the rent collected from the mortgaged property in payment of: taxes and rates and other outgoings; outstanding sums including interest on prior encumbrances; his own commission; insurance premiums and repairs and principal; and interest due under the mortgage.

A receiver is regarded as an agent of the mortgagor and is accountable to him for the monies received and for disbursements.

The mortgagee will not be liable for any of his actions or costs of receivership (unless the bank or building society manager has been appointed as a receiver).

If the mortgagor is a limited company, file a notice of Appointment of Receiver at Companies Registry within seven days of the appointment.

A lender would normally appoint a receiver where the tenanted property was subject to the receipt of rental income.

A receiver has the power to receive rental income of the property by action, distress or otherwise, give receipts thereof (s.109 (3)), grant leases or accept surrenders using the Power of Attorney.

If a property is occupied by the mortgagor or his associates, and they are to be allowed to remain in occupation, ask them to pay an Occupation Fee. This will not give rise to any claim to a Statutory Tenancy, but allows the mortgagor to continue to trade and at the same time forward income to the lender.

3. *Foreclose*

A foreclosure order, irrespective of the amount of the debt and the value of security, deprives the mortgagor of his right of redemption of the mortgage. The right of redemption of the title to the property is transferred to the mortgagee.

A mortgagee who forecloses and becomes an owner is not accountable to the borrower, even if surplus monies are available from the sale of the property. Therefore a mortgagee need only obtain official funds to clear its outstanding liabilities. It will not be under a duty to obtain the best possible market price.

To obtain this order, consent of the court is required. It is rarely granted because of the reasons stated above. The court will usually order a sale of the property. Initially an order *nisi* will be granted by the court, but before granting this order, the court will give the mortgagor time to repay the debt. If, within six months repayment has not been made, the order becomes 'absolute' and the mortgagor's rights to redeem his property will be extinguished, thus vesting the title in the name of the mortgagee.

Once order 'absolute' is granted, the rights of subsequent mortgagees also become extinguished.

4. *Obtain possession of the mortgaged property*
This remedy is seldom exercised by the lenders, because the same effect is achieved more cheaply and without accepting onerous responsibilities by appointment of a receiver.

The reason why lenders are reluctant to exercise their rights under this remedy is that, although they can grant leases, collect rent and make payment in reduction of the debt, they are also accountable for profits received. They are liable for profits lost if they have acted negligently: *White* v *City of London Brewery Co.* [1889].

5.17.1 Methods of obtaining possession by a mortgagee

(a) *By court order*
    A lender will have to comply with the legal requirements of the court.

(b) *By agreement*
    A borrower who is in arrears may surrender the property to the lender voluntarily without the need for the lender to obtain a court order. The borrower signs a possession declaration and agrees to pay interest and capital until the property is sold.

(c) *Surrender by the borrower*
    Where no prior discussion or agreement relating to the arrears has taken place, and the borrower vacates the property without advising the lender, the lender will then sell the property.

(d) *A suspended order*
    If the borrower can satisfy the court that he is able to pay the arrears within a reasonable period, the court may grant a suspended order, in which case the lender will not have a possession order. If the terms of the suspended order are breached, then the lender may apply to the court for the order to be enforced. If the court grants an order, the lender may proceed for a warrant for possession.

(e) *Sell the property (power of sale)*
    This is the most common remedy. Under the Law of Property Act 1925, s.103 (power to sell) and s.109 (power to appoint a receiver), the power to sell only arises in the following circumstances.

    (i)   The demand for repayment has been made and the mortgagor has defaulted in payment of part or all of it for a period of three months. Because most mortgage forms state that monies secured by the mortgage are payable on due demand, the provisions of s.103 are excluded, giving the lender an immediate power of sale or power to appoint a receiver.

(ii) As a charge will be by way of legal mortgage, an order for sale from the court is not required unless the lending falls within the regulated agreement under the Consumer Credit Act 1974, and provided that the property is empty and no chattel assets remain.

(iii) Interest under the mortgage is two months in arrears.

(iv) The mortgagor has breached some of the covenants of the mortgage, other than the covenant to repay.

According to s.101 of the Law of Property Act 1925, a mortgagee has power to sell the mortgaged property provided that: the mortgage is executed as a deed; the mortgagee is not prevented by the deed from using the power (or in case of a building society, the rules); and the mortgage debt has become due.

5.17.2 Steps to be taken by lenders when selling a property

1. Check that the mortgage is executed as a deed or in accordance with the provisions of s.1 of the Law of Property (Miscellaneous Provisions) Act 1989, enabling the bank to sell the property under s.101 of the Law of Property Act 1925. If it is not executed as a deed, obtain a court order authorising the bank to sell as mortgagee.

2. Ensure that demand for repayment has been made on the mortgagor (and that the mortgagor is in arrears of the mortgage payment in whole). Usually bank mortgage forms provide a clause enabling them to enforce their security on demand. Even if this clause is not provided by virtue of s.103 of the Law of Property Act 1925, the bank can exercise its power of sale (see below) upon the customer's default, provided the bank has made formal demand.

3. Consider the problems of possible overriding interests. If the property is not vacant, obtain a possession order from the court and then a warrant of execution to evict the occupants if they have not vacated voluntarily within 28 days of the possession order.

In respect of a legal mortgage, a bank does not have to obtain a court order to sell, but for an equitable mortgage, a court order may be required.

4. Where there is a regulated agreement, obtain consent of court (s.126 of the Consumer Credit Act 1974).

5. Ensure that professional and qualified estate agents are instructed to act on behalf of the bank or society to sell the property.

6. Ensure that the bank acts honestly, equitably and in good faith. It must take care to sell the property at a true open market price: *Cuckmere Brick Co. Ltd v Mutual Finance Ltd* [1971].

In *Tse Kwong Lam* v *Wong Chit Sen* [1983], it was held that provided the sale is entered into in good faith and the lender has taken reasonable care to obtain the best price that can reasonably be obtained, the mortgagee under his power of sale may sell to a company in which he has an interest.

In *Parker–Tweedale* v *Dunbar Bank plc and others* [1990], it was held that when exercising its power of sale a mortgagee who is on notice of a person's beneficial interest in the mortgaged property did not owe an independent duty over and above the duty owed to the mortgagor in taking a reasonable care to obtain a proper price.

Another related case is *Standard Chartered Bank Ltd* v *Walker & Walker* [1982], where it was held that a receiver owes a duty of care to a mortgagor and to a guarantor.

The property may not be sold to the customer, to the bank itself (or in the case of a building society to its agents, including the selling agent), or to any employee or officer of the bank or society. Otherwise it will be considered as undersold, even if it was purchased at a price higher than the valuation: *Martinson* v *Clowes* [1882].

7.   Disclose all material facts likely to affect the prices.

8.   Ensure that the sale of the property takes place by obtaining a proper valuation, by advertising, or auction or private treaty arrangements, etc. and the property is sold at the market value: *Standard Chartered Bank* v *Walker and Walker* [1982]. Bearing in mind the decision in this case, if a bank holds a direct security and a guarantee, it (or a receiver if appointed) owes a duty of care to the mortgagor and the guarantor to obtain a reasonable market price.

If a receiver is appointed, do not interfere with his decisions. Also note that a receiver acts as an agent of the mortgagor.

9.   Do not delay or postpone the sale in anticipation of obtaining a higher price: *Bank of Cyprus (London) Ltd* v *Gill* [1980]; *China and South Sea Bank Ltd* v *Tan* [1990].

A building society selling as a mortgagee must comply with the requirement of s.13 (7) and Schedule 4 of the Building Societies Act 1986, i.e.:

(a)   exercise 'reasonable care' to obtain the best price that can be reasonably obtained. Although there is no such provision concerning sale by banks and other mortgagees, their position is not very different from that of building societies;

(b)   send to the mortgagor a notice by recorded delivery at his last known address, containing the prescribed particulars of sale within 28 days from the completion date of sale.

Building societies and other mortgagees are not under any obligation to 'nurse' the property until such time as it obtains a better price: *Reliance Permanent Building Society* v *Harwood Stamper* [1944].

Apply the sales proceeds as follows.

(a) Towards expenses of sale and for repayment of mortgage liabilities, plus interest.

(b) Payment to any subsequent mortgagee. Check if the lender has received a notice of subsequent mortgage. In case of unregistered land, carry out a search at the Land Charges Registry and remit surplus monies to the subsequent mortgagee. If there is no subsequent mortgage, send surplus funds to the borrower, or on his written instructions to a specified person. If the borrower is bankrupt then send surplus funds to the trustee in bankruptcy (if there is one).

In case of registered land, search at a Land Registry is not necessary because the Land Registry will advise the prior mortgagee of subsequent entries if the banks' right to make further advances has been recorded in the register.

If a lender or mortgagee incurs loss from the sale, consider the option of recovering it: on a surrender value of an endowment policy, if assigned; or from the guarantor if he has executed a guarantee; or a claim on any insurance guarantee policy; or from the monies deposited as security for the advance made by the mortgagee and recover it from the borrower.

5.18 REMEDIES OF AN EQUITABLE MORTGAGEE

1. Under hand
As an equitable mortgagee, a lender can pursue the following remedies.

(a) Sue the mortgagor for recovery of interest and capital.

(b) Foreclose in the same way as a legal mortgagee.

(c) The mortgagor would have signed a memorandum of deposit, undertaking to execute the legal mortgage when called upon to do so. If he executes such a mortgage, then the lender will have all the remedies available to a legal mortgagee. If the lender does not, then the mortgagee cannot sell the property or appoint a receiver or enter into possession without reference to the court.

2. Under seal

If the bank's mortgage is executed by deed it will have a power of sale and power to appoint a receiver (s.101 Law of Property Act 1925).

If an equitable mortgage executed by deed is held, the bank will have all the remedies available to a legal mortgagee.

The bank will have power to convey the legal title to the purchaser without permission of the court: *Re White Rose Cottage* [1965], if its mortgage incorporates:

(a) a power of attorney clause whereby the mortgagee appoints a senior bank official to act as his agent to sell or grant leases or execute a legal mortgage on the property; and

(b) a declaration of trust clause whereby the mortgagor confirms he holds the property in a trust for the bank (see page 119).

5.19 REMEDIES OF A SECOND MORTGAGEE

Second mortgagees have similar remedies to those available to first mortgagees but are subject to certain restrictions.

1. Sue

Second mortgagees may sue the mortgagor if he fails to repay his debt.

2. Sell the property

Second mortgagees may sell the property without recourse to the first mortgagee, but subject to the standing first mortgage. This is rarely done. In practice a second mortgagee either persuades the first mortgagee to join in the sale, utilising the sale proceeds to discharge both mortgagees' debts, or pays off the first mortgagee if it agrees to do so and rank as a first mortgagee. If the first mortgagee does not co-operate, then application to the court must be made to pay off the first mortgage, so that the property may then be sold without any outstanding encumbrance (s. 50 Law of Property Act 1925). Second mortgagees cannot sell the property without a court order if the mortgage is not executed by deed.

3. Appointment of receiver

A second mortgagee can appoint a receiver provided that his mortgage is executed by deed and does not exclude such a power. Leasing powers may be delegated. A receiver must utilise all the rents received in accordance with the second mortgagee's instructions.

If the second mortgage is not by deed, the mortgagee will have to refer to the court for an appointment of a receiver.

4. Possession of property

If the first mortgagee has not taken possession of the mortgaged property or if a receiver has not been appointed, then under the second mortgage, a second mortgagee may take possession of the mortgaged property.

The second mortgagee will be accountable to the mortgagor for rents and profits on the footing of 'wilful default' under an obligation to pay rents and, if the mortgagor is in arrears, pay outstanding interest on the first mortgage.

5.20   REMEDIES OF A SUB-MORTGAGEE

1.   Sue

A sub-mortgagee may sue for the debt.

2.   Sale of the debt

A sub-mortgagee may exercise the power of sale and sell the mortgage debt itself if any other purchaser can be found. This power can be exercised when default on the sub-mortgage occurs, even if no default had occurred under the head mortgage.

5.20.1   Powers conferred by the head mortgage

If default occurs under both the head mortgage and the sub-mortgage, the sub-mortgagee. may exercise powers conferred by the head mortgage. The powers available must always be checked.

6 Securities given by companies

All references in this chapter are to the Companies Act 1985 (CA 1985) unless otherwise stated.

(a) Companies Act 1985 (CA 1985): This Act updated and consolidated earlier statutes.
(b) Companies Act 1989 (CA 1989): This Act has made provision for certain sections of CA 1985 to be amended or replaced, or added.
(c) Insolvency Act 1986 (IA 1986): This Act removed all those matters relating to insolvent companies and individuals and the winding up of solvent companies from CA 1985.

The most important amendments made by CA 1989 are:

(a) the abolition of the *ultra vires* doctrine; and
(b) the changes relating to the procedure for the registration and cancellation of registered charges.

6.1 COMPANY CHARGES

The two types of charges which a company may create are (1) a fixed charge and (ii) a floating charge. This section and the section relating to the registration and cancellation of charges by companies take account of the changes brought in by the Companies Act 1989.

6.1.1 Advantages of a floating charge

The advantages of floating charges are:

(a) They are flexible and effective.
(b) The value of the bank's security is enhanced as the company has freedom to deal with its assets freely and utilise other lines of credit.
(c) By allowing the company to continue to trade, the administrative receiver may be able to realise the assets effectively.

A floating charge holder may block the appointment of an administrator receiver (IA 1986, s. 9(3)).

An administrator, when appointed, would require the court's permission to dispose of an asset subject to a fixed charge, but it would not require such a consent in respect of an asset subject to a floating charge.

(d)   Floating charges can be made to cover all or part of the debtor's or undertaking.

(e)   They enable a debenture holder to appoint a receiver and a manager or the whole undertaking.

6.1.2   Defects of a floating charge

When lending against the security of a debenture or a floating charge on its own, lenders should bear in mind their potential defects as they are equitable charges.

Despite the following disadvantages of the floating charge as security, where the main assets of a company constitute stock in trade and debtors, lenders may accept them as   security by carrying out regular valuations and retaining a sufficient margin.

1.   Twelve months' rule

If a floating charge is taken as a security within 12 months of the commencement of winding up, or a petition for an administration order, or if the company is unable to pay its debts at the time it is given, or becomes unable to pay the debt as a result of the transaction, it may be invalid as security.

Past advances are not covered, unless the company was solvent at the time of creation of the charge. However, *Clayton's* case will operate in favour of the lender, the debt outstanding at the date of the charge will be reduced by future credits, whilst new advances created by future debits will be secured by the floating charge: *Re Thomas Mortimer Ltd* [1925] and *Re Yeovil Glove Co Ltd* [1965].

A floating charge which has crystallised will, under s. 259 of IA 1986, be postponed even to preferential debts arising after crystallisation.

2.   Priority of preferential creditors

If a company is wound up or an administrative receiver appointed, the preferential creditors (PAYE, VAT, wages, etc.) will rank ahead of a floating charge holder (ss. 40 and 175, IA 1986), but not ahead of the creditors who have a fixed charge on the company's assets. For this reason it is preferable to obtain a fixed charge over book debts.

If a lender has a suspicion that the company is likely to go into liquidation, a separate account should be opened for wages and salaries in order to maximise the claims, by preventing the operation of the rule in *Clayton's* case. Present limits are £800 per person, spread over a period of the previous four months.

A guarantor of a preferential debt who discharges it will have the same priority as the creditor would have had if the guarantor had not paid it: *Re Lamplugh Iron Ore Co.*[1927].

(c) *Subsequent fixed charges*

Since a fixed charge attaches a property when it is created and a floating charge when it crystallises, if another lender obtains a subsequent fixed legal or equitable charge over the company's assets, which are already subject to a bank's floating charge, then provided that the subsequent chargee had no notice of any 'negative pledge' clause incorporated in the bank's floating charge, he will have priority on the fixed assets covered by the floating charge: *Wheatley* v *Silkstone and Haigh Moor Coal Co.*[1883].

To retain their priority lenders incorporate, in the debenture form, a negative pledge clause precluding the company from creating subsequent charges over the same property which will rank in priority to, or *pari passu* with, the floating charge.

To qualify as a fixed charge, the charge must incorporate the following.

(a)   Restrictions on dealings in the ordinary course of business.

(b)   In the case of book debts, restrictions preventing the company from collecting in the debts on its own account: *Siebe Gorman & Co. Ltd* v *Barclays Bank Ltd* [1979]; *Re Keenan Bros. Ltd* [1986]; *Re Brightlife Ltd* [1986]. In the case of *William Gaskell Group Ltd & Others* v *Highley & Another* [1993], it was held that on making an assignment, thereby transferring the benefit of a debenture from the bank to the assignee (Waldis Investments), the charge on book debts remained fixed and did not become floating. The decision was in line with the decision in *Siebe Gorman & Co. Ltd* v *Barclays Bank Ltd* [1979], which highlighted that the decision in each case was dependent on the constructions of a clause in a particular debenture.

4.   *Retention of title clauses*

The company is free to deal with its assets, so that by the time the debenture holder intervenes, there may be few assets left due to unprofitable trading. Where its memorandum of association so authorises, the company may dispose of all its assets in exchange for shares in another company: *Re Borax Company* [1901].

If monies are to be advanced to a buyer (company) mostly against the security of stock, the lender must establish the total value of stock supplied to him on credit, which is subject to a 'retention of title clause' (known as the Romalpa clause), for example, a conditional sale agreement incorporating a clause that the goods will remain the supplier's property until he has been paid in full and if the buyer has sold the goods, the original supplier will be entitled to the proceeds of sale.

The lender should consider the following issues concerning Romalpa clauses:

(a)　If the goods are resold by the company, the company will hold the sale proceeds as the constructive trustee of the seller's property in possession of the company.

(b)　If goods are used by the company in the process of manufacture, the company will pay a proportion of the manufactured product.

Problems relating to retention of title have been highlighted in *Aluminium Industrie Vaasen B.V.* v *Romalpa Aluminium Ltd* [1976]. In this case the Court of Appeal held that a supplier may retain title to his goods delivered to the buyer until he was paid, and that if the goods are resold by the company, it will hold the sale proceeds as constructive trustee of the supplier's property in the hands of the company.

Bear in mind that the value of goods shown in the balance sheet of the company may be subject to retention clauses, and that an administrative receiver appointed under the debenture will not be able to sell them on behalf of the bank.

A buyer may not be required to register a Romalpa clause, because it is not a charge giving rights over his own property and the property remains with the supplier until he has been paid in full: *Romalpa* case and *Armour* v *Thyssen Edelstahlwerke AG* [1991].

However, if a clause only reserves 'beneficial and equitable title' to the supplier, such a clause would constitute a charge which must be registered, because the legal title has passed to the buyer: *Re Bond Worth Ltd* [1979].

(c)　If a clause provides that:

(i)　the goods will remain the seller's property until repayment of goods in full has been made;

(ii)　the buyer may not sell the goods as principal, but must hold the proceeds of sale for the seller; and

(iii)　if the buyer will hold the goods for the seller as bailee, then registration at Companies Registry will be required, otherwise it will be considered void: *Tatung (UK) Ltd* v *Galex Telesure Ltd* [1989].

(d)　A clause stating that a title to goods which includes supplier's materials shall be held on behalf of that supplier will require registration at Companies Registry: *Re Peachdart Ltd* [1984].

Lenders should also be aware of the following cases relating to retention clauses:

(i) *Clough Mill Ltd* v *Martin* [1984]: in this case it was held that goods can be recovered, if they are in the possession of the buyer and are still in their original state, so that they can be identified, and provided the seller's agreement incorporates a retention of title clause.

(ii) *Hendy Lennox (Industrial Engines) Ltd* v *Grahame Puttick Ltd* [1984]: where goods sent by the supplier have been used in a manufacturing process, the position will depend upon whether the goods supplied can be identified.

(iii) *Borden (UK) Ltd* v *Scottish Timber Products Ltd* [1979]: if goods have been admixed and have lost their original identity, they can be recovered if the retention clause incorporates a claim on the finished product.

(iv) *Re Andrabell Ltd* [1984]: it was held that, if the terms upon which a person received money were that he was bound to keep it separate, either in a bank or elsewhere, and to hand the money as a separate fund to the person entitled to it, then he was a trustee of that money and must hand it over to the person who is cestui que trust.

Whether sales agreements incorporating Romalpa clauses require registration at Companies Registry or not will depend on the wordings of the clauses and when the CA 1989 registration requirements come into force. In *Re Weldtech Equipment Ltd* [1990], Hoffmann J. decided that s. 395 of CA 1985 applied to all charges created by companies registered in England, even where the law governing the instrument which created the charge was that of a different jurisdiction.

5. Running down of assets

A company may, without the bank's knowledge, sell the stock and pay the receipts from the debtors to the other pressing, unsecured creditors, thus diminishing the value of the bank's floating charge.

To minimise the risk, obtain regular statements from the company of its current assets and liabilities to ensure that the required margin is maintained. Value the charged assets on a going concern basis. Compare the figures given by the company with the audited figures.

6. Seizure of assets by landlords or creditors

The company's goods may be seized and sold by a judgment creditor, or the landlord if rent is owing to him. If goods are sold before crystallisation of the bank's floating charge, they will be entitled to retain the money.

6.1.3 Priorities of charges

When taking security of a floating charge, provided that both the creditors have not entered into any prior agreement thereby varying the rules, priority will be determined in accordance with the following guidelines:

1. Fixed Charges

Fixed charges rank ahead of floating charges.

For legal (fixed) charges, priorities will rank in accordance with:

(i) the date of creation, provided registration within 21 days at Companies Registry has been effected;

(ii) provided a subsequent legal chargee had no notice of an existing equitable charge, he will gain priority over an earlier equitable (fixed) charge in respect of the same property. Because the earlier charge would have been registered, the subsequent chargee would be on constructive notice of the earlier charge.

(iii) Where two floating charges are given over the general assets of a company, priority will be determined in the order of creation, but if a floating charge over a specific asset is created, then it will rank ahead of an existing floating charge over the entire assets and undertakings.

A charge which is not registered at Companies Registry within the prescribed time limit will lose priority over other valid charges.

If details of the negative pledge clauses are filed with the Registrar of Companies so that an inspection would reveal them, such registration is deemed to give actual notice to the lender of a subsequent charge because lenders, before advancing money, normally make a search at Companies Registry.

However, despite a negative pledge clause, where a loan against an asset has been agreed before purchase or completion, e.g. by a building society, the society's legal mortgage will attach to the property when the company acquires it and will prevail over the floating charge: *Re·Connolly Bros. Ltd (No.2)* [1912], approved by the House of Lords in *Abbey National Building Society* v *Cann* [1990]. Had there been a moment of time when the company had the unencumbered asset, the floating charge would have attached to this after acquired property and have priority.

2. Floating charges over book debts

The rule in *Dearle* v *Hall* [1828] cannot be applicable to floating charges over book debts, because a floating charge holder, having impliedly consented to the subsequent fixed charge, cannot rank ahead by serving notice to the debtor after crystallisation of the charge.

3. Future property

An agreement to give security over future property does not create a security interest, but creates a present security right, although there is no property to which anything can be attached.

4. Fixed charges over future book debts

A fixed charge over future book debts has priority over later fixed charges, floating charges and preferential creditors.

Bank debenture forms usually incorporate a clause creating a fixed charge over debts already owned by the debtor, and a specific assignment over general book debts and other debts owned at present or which the company may own in future, thus creating a fixed charge over outstanding debtors. This charge will have priority over preferential creditors and over a floating charge.

An advantage of a floating charge is that an administrative receiver appointed under the charge has power to dispose even of property subject to another chargee's fixed security.

In a winding up, a bank is entitled to apply its fixed charge proceeds as it wishes between preferential and non-preferential claims: *Re William Hall (Contractors) Ltd* [1967]. However, according to the decision in *Re Unit 2 Windows* [1985], a creditor when applying Statutory Set Off Rule 4.90 must set off preferential and non-preferential debts rateably against credit balances.

6.2 CIRCUMSTANCES WHICH WOULD RENDER A CHARGE VOID

A fixed or a floating charge may be challenged and held as void against the liquidator on the following grounds.

1. Non-registration (delivery of particulars) of charges within 21 days of creation (applicable to both fixed and floating charges).

2. Charges given in *ultra vires* transactions.

3. Charges created in an irregular or unauthorised manner by the board of directors.

4. The continuation of the account, whereby the original debt is discharged because of the running account, unless the security is a continuing one (which

usually it will be: *Clayton's* case). This will apply to fixed and floating charges.
5.   The 12-month rule regarding floating charges (s. 245, IA 1986).

(a)   Time

If a floating charge is created within 12 months before granting of an administration order or liquidation of a company, it will be automatically void. Application to the court is not required. The charge will be invalid but the debt will not. In case of a charge created in favour of a person connected with the company (for example, a director), the time period is two years instead of 12 months, ending with the onset of insolvency.

(b)   Insolvent company

The rule applies only if the company is insolvent when the charge is given (i.e., its liabilities exceed its assets, s. 123, IA 1986).

(c)   No consideration

A charge is valid if taken as a security in respect of payment of monies, or supply of goods to the company, at the time of or after the creation of the charge, or for a reduction or satisfaction of company's debts, together with any interest on these: *Re F and E Stanton Ltd* [1927]. It is also valid if, when the advance is made, an unconditional promise is given to provide security at some future time and this is done.

If the advance is made after creation of a floating charge, but utilised for payment of an unsecured debt (of the same chargee) prevailing at the time of creation of the charge, the charge will be void as security for the later loan and will not be considered as a new loan.

(d)   *Clayton's* case

In this class of case the bank will benefit by the rule in *Clayton's* case because if the account is turned over subsequent to the charge, that debt at the time of winding up will represent a new debt, the old debt having been discharged: *Re Yeovil Glove Co. Ltd* [1965].
6.   Preferences (ss. 238–240, IA 1986).

For the purposes of s. 239 and s. 241, a company gives a preference to a person if:

(a)(i)   that person is one of the company's creditors or a surety or guarantor for any of the company's debts or other liabilities; and

(ii)   the company does anything or suffers anything to be done which (in either case) has the effect of putting that person into a position which, in the event of the company going into insolvent liquidation, will be better than the position he would have been in if that action had not been taken: *Re MC Bacon Ltd* [1990].

According to s. 435 a person is 'associated' with another if he is a spouse, relative, a spouse's relative or a spouse of either of the relatives; a partner or relative of a partner; employer or employee; or a trustee.

(b) The preference must be given within six months before winding up or two years for connected persons (s. 240(1) and s. 341(1), IA 1986).

Other cases related to preference are: *Re Paraguassu Steam Tramway Co. Ltd* [1874]; *Re M. Kushler Ltd* [1943]; *Liquidator of West Mercia Safety Wear Ltd* v *Dodd* [1988]; *Re FLE Holdings Ltd* [1967].

(c) The company is insolvent at the time of preference.

(d) If the company pays off its debt to the bank so that the guarantor is discharged.

7. *Undervalues*

For the purposes of ss. 238–240, IA 1986, the 'transactions at an undervalue' apply:

(a) When the company is insolvent at the time of transaction.

(b) A transaction at an undervalue is one in which the company or a person makes a gift or enters into a transaction receiving no, or significantly less, consideration than he provides (ss. 238 and 339, IA 1986): *Re Kumar (a bankrupt)* [1993].

(c) (b) above must occur within two years of the winding up.

(d) The court can make an order upsetting the transaction, but not if the transaction was bona fide for the purposes of the company's business, and if, when it was done, there were reasonable grounds to think the company would be benefited.

6.3   INTERESTED DIRECTORS

If the bank has already obtained the directors' guarantees as security for the company's liabilities, and if the bank subsequently takes another security from the company, thereby reducing the extent of directors' liability, they will be considered as 'interested', and the security will be held as void against a liquidator: *Victors Ltd* v *Lingard* [1927].

To protect against this, the bank should obtain an executed debenture first, and then obtain the guarantees of the directors, so that the debenture is dated before the date of the executed guarantee. Where both are required, the bank should obtain them simultaneously.

Prior to the new provisions of CA 1989, banks used to inspect the company's articles to check if the 'interested' directors were allowed to vote on the contract in which they were interested. If the articles were silent on voting powers, banks used to protect themselves by obtaining:

(a) a resolution from the disinterested quorum of directors authorising giving of the additional security; or

(b) amendment of the company's articles to enable the interested directors to vote; or

(c) a shareholders' resolution (even if the shareholders were the interested directors) in a general meeting authorising the charging of the additional security.

The 'interested' directors were allowed to vote if the articles specifically mentioned that the company had adopted Article 94(b) under CA 1985, or Article 84(2) under CA 1948.

When the problems of interested directors exist, a bank has the following options:

(i) to obtain the company's articles and to follow (a), (b) and (c) above; or

(ii) to rely on the director's confirmation that they have rectified the position and taken necessary steps, or to rely on the protection available in CA 1989.

However, at the time of writing, as the new changes are still not in force, it is safer to follow the old procedure as outlined in (a), (b) and (c) until these new rules come into force.

6.4 *ULTRA VIRES* RULE

Section 108 of CA 1989 has amended s. 35 of CA 1985, and the *ultra vires* rule in respect of transactions between the company and third parties (for example, its bankers) has been abolished.

However, to seek the protection provided a bank acts in good faith with the company, any transaction entered into between the bank and the company will be binding on the company, even if the stated powers of the company or its directors are exceeded.

Because of the uncertainty, and due to ambiguities in the new Act some banks still continue to request a copy of the memorandum and articles of association for inspection.

A recent decision in *Hazell v London Borough of Hammersmith and Fulham* [1991], concerning *ultra vires* actions by a local authority, shows the need to adopt a cautious approach by examining the memorandum and articles of association.

The *ultra vires* aspect must also be considered when a company gives a guarantee to secure a loan to a third party, usually an associated company. The bank, in these circumstances, should inspect the memorandum and articles of association of each subsidiary company to check that the objects clause incorporates an express power to give guarantees, and there are no other conditions or restrictions on the powers of the directors to give such guarantees.

6.4.1 Memorandum of Association

Ultra vires problems appear to have been reduced by s. 110(i), CA 1989, according to which, if an objects clause allows the company 'to carry on business as a general commercial company', then the company:

(a) can carry on any trade or business whatsoever; and
(b) has power to do all such things as are incidental or conducive to the carrying on of any trade or business by it.

In the absence of the above clauses in the memorandum, a provision for a specified objects clause will be made.

6.5 REGISTRATION OF CHARGES

6.5.1 The Provisions of Part IV of CA 1989

This section on company charges and registration of charges takes account of the changes brought by CA 1989.

Section 92 – The Provisions of Part IV of CA 1989 amend the provisions of CA 1985 relating to the registration of company charges by inserting in Part XII of CA 1985 (in place of ss 395 - 408 and ss.410–423) new provisions with respect to companies registered in Great Britain. Section 93 of CA 1989 replaces ss.395 and 396 of CA 1985 with new sections specifying charges requiring registration.

6.5.2 Charges requiring registration (s.93, CA 1989)

The following sections are inserted in Part XII of CA 1985:

In this part, the new s. 395 defines the term 'charge' as any form of security interest (fixed or floating) over property, other than an interest arising by operation of law; and 'property' in the context of what is the subject of a charge, includes future property.

Charges requiring registration (in England and Wales) under this part (s. 396(1)) are:

(a) A charge on land or any interest in land excluding a charge for rent or other periodical sums issuing out of land.

(b) A charge on goods or any interest in goods (tangible moveable property other than a charge under which a chargee is entitled to possession either of the goods or the documents of title to them).

(c) A charge on intangible, moveable property (goodwill, intellectual property book debts, and uncalled share capital of the company, or calls made but not paid).

An intellectual property is any patent, trademark, service mark, registered design, copyright or design right registered or any licence under or in respect of such right. Book debts include those of the company or those assigned to the company, but exclude deposits by way of security of negotiable instruments to secure the payment of book debts and shipowner's lien.

(d) A charge for securing an issue of debentures ('issue' means a series of debentures). (A single bank debenture is not covered (s. 397).)

(e) A floating charge on the whole or part of the company's property, including floating charges over book debts. A charge upon 'contingent debt' does not require registration if it has some contingency or condition or qualification or event, so that until the condition is fulfilled or the relevant event occurs, the debt is hypothetical. Future book debts require registration, as they are not regarded as contingent: *Independent Automatic Sales Ltd* v *Knowles & Foster* [1962]. Where a bank holds a company's irrevocable authority, allowing the company's debtors to pay sums directly into the company's bank account, it will require registration, as it will create a charge over the book debts: *Re Kent & Sussex Saw Mills Ltd* [1947].

141

Charges on assets situated in Great Britain, given by a company registered overseas, but having an established place of business in the UK, must be registered at the Companies Registry within 21 days of execution. Bearing in mind the decision in the case of *Slavenburg's Bank NV* v *Intercontinental Natural Resources Ltd* [1980], it is vital that banks attempt registration, within the specified time limit, when charges over British assets by overseas registered companies are taken as security.

6.5.3 Charges not requiring registration

(a)   Charges over life policies.

(b)   A pledge over goods, even if they are released by way of trust receipt to the pledgor.

(c)   Charges over stocks and shares (unless the charge is floating).

(d)   A negotiable instrument deposited as security (for example, a bill of exchange or a cheque).

(e)   Charges over chattels, for example, charges over goods in foreign parts at sea, or goods under documents of title used in the ordinary course of business.

(f)   Since such 'rights' for example, as liens, or equitable or statutory set off, are not charges and are not created by the company, they do not require registration. But if security or title deeds are deposited with an intention of creating a security right, this equitable mortgage may require registration: *Re Molton Finance Ltd* [1967]; *Re Wallis & Simmonds (Builders) Ltd* [1975].
Reservation of title clause may require registration in relation to mixed goods but not in respect of non-mixed goods (see 6.1.2, number 4).

(g)   Deposits held by the bank as 'flawed assets' arrangements are not charges and do not need to be registered. But it is not clear whether a contractual set off clause in respect of deposits held by a bank can be regarded as a charge: *Re Charge Card Services Ltd* [1986].
Neither a lien nor a set off are registrable, as they are not charges created by a company, but are rights which arise against property through common law or statute. Charges over choses in action do not require to be registered.

(h)   A charge over existing contractual right. An Export Credits Guarantee

Department Insurance Policy (*Paul & Frank Ltd* v *Discount Bank (Overseas) Ltd* [1967]) does not require registration if no book debt exists at that time.

(i)   A guarantee given by a company to secure the debts and obligations of a third party.

6.5.4   Delivery of particulars for registration (s. 95, CA 1989)

The following sections are inserted in Part XII of CA 1985:

It is the duty of a company to deliver the prescribed particulars of the charge in the prescribed form 395 to the registrar for registration within 21 days of creation of the charge or the date of acquisition of the property, as appropriate (s. 398 (1)).

Particulars may also be delivered by another person interested in the charge, i.e. the bank (s. 398(2)).

The registrar will record the particulars of the registered charge and note the date upon which the particulars are delivered.

As a certificate of registration is no longer regarded as conclusive evidence that the provisions of registration have been complied with (in accordance with the new procedure), the registrar, after receiving the particulars, will send a copy of the particulars, indicating the date upon which they were delivered, to the company and the chargee and any other person who delivered the particulars.

The 21 days begin to run from the date of execution and acquisition, and not the date of registration or the date when the monies were lent (s. 398(1)).

Particulars of an existing charge can be either supplemented or varied by delivering further particulars to the registrar (s. 401). The covering form must be signed by the company and the chargee bank.

6.5.5   Failure to deliver

Where a charge is created by a company and no prescribed particulars in the prescribed form are delivered for registration within the period of 21 days after the date of the charge's creation, the charge is void against:

(a)   an administrator or liquidator of the company, and

(b)   any person who for value acquires an interest in, or right over, property subject to the charge, where the relevant event occurs after the creation of the charge, whether before or after the end of the 21-day period (s.399(i)).

A subsequent lender who takes a charge, which is registered within 21 days of its creation, will gain priority over the previous charge not correctly registered, even if the subsequent lender had actual notice of the prior unregistered charge.

6.5.6 Late delivery of particulars

If the charge is not registered within 21 days of its creation, it is not automatically void, although it will be void if a 'relevant event' occurs after the creation of the charge but before delivery of the particulars.

If the 'relevant event' has not occurred, the charge which is not registered within 21 days can be perfected by late delivery under s. 400(1) so that it will not be void against the liquidator, administrator, or a purchaser if the 'relevant event' occurs after registration. In *Re Telomatic Ltd, Barclays Bank plc* v *Cyprus Popular Bank Ltd* [1993], an application by Barclays to register its charge at Companies Registry out of time, and subject to the proviso that its charge should have priority over subsequent chargee's (Cyprus Popular Bank) charge was refused by the court.

Section 400(2) provides that a charge registered late may be void against an administrator or liquidator if, at the date of the delivery of the particulars, the company was unable to pay its debts or became unable to pay its debts as a result of the transaction, and if insolvency proceedings began, before the end of the 'relevant period'.

In *Mace Builders (Glasgow) Ltd* v *Lunn* [1986], it was held that the liquidator could not claim, from the debenture holder, the monies from the realised assets because the realisation took place before liquidation.

6.5.7 Delivery of inaccurate particulars

If the particulars sent to the registrar are inaccurate and incomplete, the charge will be void against an administrator, liquidator or a person acquiring rights in the property, to the extent that the particulars were incomplete or inaccurate (s. 402(1)).

The charge will be void against the above parties where a 'relevant event' occurs at the time the particulars are incomplete and inaccurate, unless otherwise ordered by the court, because of an application made by the bank (s. 402 (2)).

The relevant event is defined in s. 399(2) and its applicability as regards omission and errors is set out in s.402(3) as follows:

(a)   The commencement of insolvency proceedings so that the charge is void against an administrator or liquidator unless the court decides that the charge is effective, as against an administrator or liquidator of the company, if it is satisfied:

    (i)   that the error or omission is unlikely to have misled an unsecured lender in such a way as to have materially prejudiced him; or

    (ii)   that no person became an unsecured creditor of the company at the time when the particulars were incomplete or inaccurate (s. 402 (4)).

(b)   The court may order that the charge is effective as against a person acquiring an interest in or right over property subject to the charge if it is satisfied that he did not rely, in connection with the acquisition, on registered particulars which were incomplete or inaccurate in a relevant respect (s.402(5)).

If a charge becomes void due to incompleteness or inaccuracy, the whole of the sum secured by the charge is payable immediately on demand.

Any mistake in the particulars registered will, for the time being, have to be rectified by court order. A reduction in the amount secured will require registration of a Memorandum of Charge Ceasing to affect the company's property and an increase in the amount secured, or change in the property charged, will require the registration of a new charge. According to CA 1989 these charges can be effected without referring to the court, by filing supplementary particulars, signed on behalf of the company and the bank (s. 401).

6.6 DEBENTURES

A debenture can be described as a document which creates a debt, or acknowledges a debt, or promises to lend money, thereby creating a debt. A debenture provides for security to be given in respect of the monies lent.

Bank debenture forms usually cover both a fixed and a floating charge over a company's assets, owned now or in future.

A debenture may be expressed as a security for all monies owed by the company to the chargee (an 'all moneys' debenture), or it may be a security for a limited sum (a 'fixed sum' debenture). Because of some of the disadvantages of a 'fixed sum' debenture, banks seldom accept them as a security.

Bank debenture forms are usually 'all monies' debentures, creating:

(a)   a fixed first charge over a company's real property, goodwill, uncalled capital;

(b)   a specific equitable charge over any real property which the company

145

may acquire in the future, and which is not actually detailed in the schedule, and charged as a legal mortgage in the debenture; and

(c)   a first floating charge over the remainder of all the assets and undertakings of the company, whatsoever and wheresoever situated.

The two types of charges a company may create are fixed and floating charges.

6.6.1   Fixed (or specific) charge

A fixed charge may be expressed to cover:

(a)   a legal or equitable mortgage over a company's freehold or leasehold land and properties, and on its fixed plant and machinery;

(b)   goodwill, uncalled capital, patents and trademarks;

(c)   a fixed charge over its book debts, debtors and other debts arising in regard to the company's usual business, both owing at present and falling due in future (equitable mortgage);

(d)   freehold and leasehold properties, plant and machinery, fixed thereto, which the company may acquire in future (by way of equitable mortgage).

In respect of (c) and (d) mentioned above, the company can only create a fixed equitable charge over:

(i)   future book debts and other debts, until such time when the debts arise and become due and owing; and
(ii)   future freehold or leasehold property and plant or machinery fixed thereto, until such time as the company acquires legal ownership of such property.

Banks' debenture forms include a clause creating a fixed, but equitable mortgage to cover this. Some forms may also have a clause requiring the company to inform the bank when future property is acquired and to deposit with it documents of title relating thereto; and that the company agrees to execute a legal mortgage in favour of the bank in respect of either future debts which fall due or future property when acquired.

The validity and effectiveness of a fixed charge over book debts was confirmed in *Siebe Gorman and Co. Ltd* v *Barclays Bank Ltd* [1979]. The court held that the validity and its effectiveness of the charge would depend on the construction of the clauses in the debenture. This was reaffirmed in the case of *William Gaskell Group Ltd & Others* v *Highley and Another* [1993], as discussed in 6.1.2 and in *New Bullas Trading Ltd* [1994].

According to the decision in *Barclays Bank plc* v *Willowbrook International Ltd* [1987], any person who knowingly assists a company in diverting book debts which should be paid to that company's bank in accordance with the provisions of a fixed charge, or who knowingly receives book debts which are subject to such a fixed charge, is liable to account as a constructive trustee.

A credit balance held in a bank account is not regarded as book debt, although a fixed charge may be created: *Re Brightlife Ltd* [1986].

6.6.2 Floating charge

A bank's debenture creates a floating charge over all remaining assets of the company which are not specifically charged to the bank under its fixed charge; for example, stock, work in progress, plant, machinery and tools, cash, other debts and book debts, if not already covered under its fixed charge, are included. In *Re Yorkshire Woolcombers Association* [1903], the nature and characteristics of a floating charge were defined as:

(a)   present security affecting all the assets of the company, but not a specific security;

(b)   the company can deal with the assets and dispose of them in the ordinary course of business, until the occurrence of a certain event which crystallises it into a fixed charge;

(c)   the assets change from time to time in the ordinary course of business until an event occurs in the future.

6.6.3 Events which crystallise the floating charge

The company is free to deal with the assets under its floating charge in the ordinary course of business, until they become 'fixed' or 'crystallise' upon the occurrence of a certain event; for example, when the terms of the debenture are breached and the bank takes action by appointing a receiver, or the company defaults in payment of interest: *Re Brightlife Ltd* [1986].

147

The floating charge crystallises when:

(a)   the company enters liquidation compulsorily or voluntarily;

(b)   in accordance with the clause in the form, when demand for repayment of the debt is made, and the company defaults; i.e. the charge pre-crystallises and becomes fixed prior to the appointment of a receiver or commencement of winding up;

(c)   the bank appoints an administrative receiver;

(d)   the company ceases business (*Re Woodroffes (Musical Instruments) Ltd* [1985]), or disposes of its entire undertaking or assets for the purpose of ceasing to trade;

(e)   when crystallisation of another floating charge causes the company to cease trading;

(f)   a distress levy by execution issued (except garnishee summons) by the landlord.

6.7   CLAUSES IN THE BANKS' STANDARD DEBENTURE FORM

Clauses found in standard bank mortgage forms have already been discussed in Chapter 5. The following specific clauses are also included in the debenture form.

1.   The debenture is in respect of all liabilities of the company, whether alone or jointly, for present or future or contingent liabilities.

2.   The company undertakes to pay on demand and s. 103 of the Law of Property Act 1925 will not apply, so that the bank has power of sale and can appoint a receiver if the company defaults.

3.   A provision for appointing an administrative receiver or a receiver or manager, who will act as the bank's agent though the bank will not be liable for the administrative receiver's acts. A clause also outlines the administrative receiver's right to receive a certain percentage (usually 5%) remuneration from the realisation proceeds of the company's assets, in priority to the debenture holder or preferential creditor.

4.   The company creates a first legal fixed charge on the scheduled mortgaged property and fixed machinery, and a first fixed equitable charge over all other company properties owned now or in future. In respect of land the company undertakes to deposit all title deeds to the bank as security and, in case of

equitable charge on the property, to execute a legal charge if called upon to do so.

5.   A fixed charge over uncalled capital, shares in and securities of subsidiaries, goodwill and book debts (present and future), and a floating charge over the company's 'undertaking', and all other assets held at present or which may be acquired later.

By incorporating a Siebe Gorman clause, a company undertakes to pay all receipts into its account with the bank and not to assign, sell or factor without the bank's consent.

6.   Some bank debenture forms also include a clause whereby a company agrees to keep a certain margin of the ratio of assets for the borrowing and to inform the bank when such a margin falls below the agreed level giving the bank the right to appoint an administrative receiver in this event.

7.   The company agrees to ensure all the buildings, plant, machinery, fixtures and stock are insured with a reputable insurance company of the bank's choice, to pay premiums on due dates and produce receipts to the bank. The bank also acquires the power to insure when necessary and debit the company's account.

8.   A clause prohibiting dealings with charged debts with the exception of paying monies into the bank's account and, if requested by the bank, to execute an assignment.

9.   The negative pledge clause restricting creation of lien or security or any fixed charge which would rank equally (*pari passu*) with or in priority to the floating charge.

10.   A 'crystallisation' or 'realisation' clause, outlining circumstances in which the bank's debt will be repayable and the security enforceable (see 6.6.3).

11.   A clause stipulating the distribution of the proceeds of realisation.

12.   A clause appointing the bank, under the irrevocable power of attorney clause, as an agent, to do the necessary acts to enforce the debenture, and to appoint other agents as substitutes for the bank.

13.   Where the property is charged, the company undertakes to repair, maintain, insure and authorises the bank to remedy this if the company fails to do so. It agrees not to accept leases or surrender of leases without the bank's consent.

14.   It agrees that it will repay all its debts, and advise the bank if and when there are any proceedings against the company.

15.   It agrees that the debenture is in addition to, and not in substitution of, any other security. It also gives the bank a right to combine accounts where credit balances are held elsewhere.

16.   Clauses dealing with the making of demand.

17. Recent debenture forms may include and refer to some of the statutory powers in Schedule 1 of IA 1986.

18. The company undertakes to provide balance sheets and accounts on demand or at regular intervals.

6.8   GENERAL PROCEDURE FOR TAKING A FIRST FIXED CHARGE GIVEN BY A LIMITED COMPANY

The general procedure for taking a first fixed charge given by a company (for its own liabilities) are as follows. As the *ultra vires* rule has been abolished, some banks do not consider it necessary to follow the first two steps listed below.

1. Inspect the memorandum to check the following:

    (a)   The company's borrowing powers i.e. the amount of the loan is *intra vires*.

    (b)   The objects clause to make sure that the requested use is *intra vires*.

    (c)   The company is allowed to give security.

2. Inspect the articles to check the following.

    (a)   The borrowing powers of the directors are adequate. Ensure that the amount of the loan is *intra vires* and, if not, that the necessary rectification is effected.

    (b)   Whether the interested directors can vote in respect of the contract in which they are interested. If 1948 Table A (Art. 84(2)(b)) or the 1985 Table A (Art. 94(b)) are mentioned in the articles, the director will be allowed to vote on a transaction even if this effects his or her liability as a guarantor. But to qualify for this, the directors must give notice of their interest in accordance with s. 317.

It is important to check whether there are interested directors, especially in cases where they have already charged their own security for the company's liabilities and are subsequently charging company's security to reduce their liability: *Victors Ltd* v *Lingard* [1927]. This will also apply in cases where a bank takes cross guarantees or inter-company guarantees which have common directors.

If the articles do not authorise the interested directors to vote, obtain a resolution by an independent quorum of directors, or by a general meeting of the company where directors would vote as shareholders, or ask the company to alter its articles thus permitting them to vote.

(c)   The method in which the bank's charge or documents should be executed, i.e. under hand or seal.

3.   Carry out a search at Companies Registry to ensure that the company has not charged the security offered to the bank elsewhere, and that there are no other charges or adverse entries against the company affecting the bank's security.

4.   Obtain deposit of the documents being charged, and the deposit of insurance policies where appropriate, with the bank's interest noted in the policy.

5.   Obtain a copy of the board resolution (duly certified by the Chairman and Secretary) authorising the transaction, detailing the security being charged and authorising the giving of security or guarantee. Either ensure that the resolution is validly passed in respect to powers, quorum and interested directors, or that the bank may rely on the rule in *Turquand's* case: *Royal British Bank* v *Turquand* [1856].

6.   Arrange for the mortgage form to be dated, signed and sealed in accordance with the requirements of the articles of association, i.e. under hand or seal and in accordance with 2. and 5. above. The mortgage must be sealed by the bank where necessary.

7.   Send the prescribed particulars of charge for registration at Companies Registry on form 395 within 21 days of the creation of the charge. Unless regulations, which may be made by the Secretary of State otherwise require, it is not necessary to send the original charge form (s. 413 (2)).

8.   The registrar will issue a certificate of filing.

9.   Carry out a search at Companies Registry again to check if the record of the charge has been correctly entered.

(For equitable charges follow the same procedure except that under 6. a memorandum of deposit or form of equitable charge should be obtained.)

10.   If a debenture is taken as a security:

(a)   Also value the security from the details available from the current balance sheet.

(b)   Ask the company to lodge an insurance policy covering the assets charged; i.e. buildings, plant, machinery, stock, etc. Give notice to the insurance company, asking for the bank's interest to be noted.

(c)   Obtain premium receipts and diarise future premium dates.

11.   Check the *Gazette* for any entries recorded against the borrower company, or against the company or companies charging or giving the security which might affect the bank's security.

6.9   GUARANTEES GIVEN BY LIMITED COMPANIES

The procedure given here is based on the assumption that the lenders will continue to inspect the company's memorandum and articles of association, and not rely on the 'new provisions' of ss. 35A and 35B of CA 1985 provided by s. 108 of CA 1989.

1.   Carry out a status enquiry search on the guarantor company, if the company's account is not held at the branch.

2.   Follow steps 1., 2., 3., 5. and 6. in section 6.8.

3.   Examine the memorandum of association to determine if an express power to give a guarantee exists. If it does not clearly specify express power to give guarantees, ask the company to alter its memorandum by special resolution.

4.   Examine the articles of association to ascertain the manner in which the guarantee is required to be executed.

Note:

(a)   Although a trading company has an implied power to borrow, it does not have an implied power to give guarantees.

(b)   The power to guarantee contracts entered into by the third parties is sufficient.

(c)   The power to 'subsidise or otherwise assist' is considered sufficient: *Re Friary Holroyd and Healys Breweries Ltd* [1992].

(d)   Inclusion of a clause to the effect that 'the company shall have power to do all such other things as are incidental or conducive to the attainment of the above objects or any of them' is not sufficient, unless a specific clause in the main objects clause authorises the giving of guarantees. If the guarantee given is *ultra vires*, ask the company to amend the memorandum by special resolution.

(e)   An ancillary power to the main objects clause cannot be enforced if the end product is detrimental to the company's principal business activity: *Rolled Steel Products (Holdings) Ltd* v *British Steel Corporation* [1986].

If there are any interested directors, ascertain if they are allowed to vote in respect of the transaction in which they have a personal interest: *Victors Ltd* v *Lingard* [1927].

6.10   INTER-COMPANY AND CROSS GUARANTEES

1.   If the bank has taken security of an inter-company guarantee, where the companies have common directors, the same considerations outlined in steps 1., 2. and 5. in section 6.8 will apply. The memorandum and articles of association of each company must be examined, searches at Companies Registry against each company must be made, and charging resolution of the companies charging the properties must also be obtained.

2.   If a company proposes to give a guarantee in respect of a loan to another company (usually a subsidiary, or an associated company, or its holding company) – for example, where a holding company borrows against a charge on its own assets and also against the security of guarantees of its subsidiaries, articles of association of each subsidiary company should be examined to see if they provide an express power to give guarantees and if directors have powers to give guarantees.

3.   If the giving of the guarantee and charging company's security is for the benefit of the company (for cross guarantees and inter-company guarantees) ensure that commercial justification exists (for example, a trading relationship or for the benefit of the company): *Wallersteiner* v *Moir* [1974]. Provided an express power to give a guarantee exists, the transaction will be valid: *Charterbridge Corporation Ltd* v *Lloyds Bank Ltd* [1969].

4.   If lending is to a company's subsidiary, ensure that the bank relies on the security of a binding guarantee and not on an unenforceable Letter of Comfort: *Kleinwort Benson Ltd* v *Malaysia Mining Corporation Berhad* [1989].

5.   Carry out a search at Companies Registry against each company to see that there are no adverse entries or charges affecting the bank's security.

6.   Obtain a certified copy of the resolution, duly signed by a Chairman and Secretary of each company, authorising the giving of a guarantee or security and specifying the method of execution.

7.   Arrange for the guarantee to be executed and give a copy of the executed guarantee to each company against their receipt.

Guarantees do not require registration at Companies Registry.

8.   Make a diary note for the renewal of status enquiry, six monthly or yearly in accordance with the bank's practice.

153

6.11 STOCKS AND SHARES

A company may own shares in another company if its memorandum of association permits, and if the memorandum of association of the company whose share it wishes to purchase allows ownership by a corporate body.

Follow the general procedure described in 6.8 and see Chapter 2.

6.12 LIFE POLICIES

Follow the same procedure described in 6.8 and see Chapter 4.

Note: A company can take a policy on the life of its executive or director, but not on its own life.

6.13 MONITORING

6.13.1 Crystallisation of floating charges

A banker whose floating charge crystallises may (when the regulations come into force), have to comply with the provisions of s. 410 of CA 1989 which are as follows:

(a) Advise the Companies Registry of:
   (i) the occurrence of events affecting the nature of the charge; and
   (ii) the action it will take in accordance with the provisions of the fixed and floating charge.

(b) To inform specified persons within a certain time limit. Until notice of a floating charge and the reason for its crystallisation are given to the Companies Registry it will be considered as ineffective.

(c) Weekly inspection of the Gazette is important. This will reveal appointments and retirements of administrative receivers and liquidators; mortgages and charges registered; satisfactions; winding up orders and presentation of winding up petitions relating to the company.

6.13.2 Deed of priority

If a bank has a security of a floating charge over a company's assets, and if the company subsequently requires finance from another bank to purchase an asset against the security of a fixed charge on that asset, the company will need the consent of the bank holding a floating charge.

If this is agreeable to the bank, then make an arrangement with the new lender bank and enter into a deed of priority which will be executed under the seal of the company, the bank and the new lender bank.

This deed of priority will give the bank a right to recover the amount of its priority, including interest and charges, and will include any variations and default clauses and details of assets which may be released from the floating charge.

6.13.3　Factoring

If the company has not created a fixed or floating charge over its assets, then it may enter into a factoring agreement.

If a company has already given a debenture to a bank creating a fixed and floating charge, the bank's consent may be required before it enters into a factoring agreement, especially in cases where a bank's debenture form contains a *pari-passu* clause. The bank will have to decide if it wants to enter into a deed of postponement in favour of the factoring company or to waive its charge over trade debtors. Usually a bank will enter into a deed of priority because the bank will be able to rely on the security of:

(a)　trade debts not factored by the factoring company; and

(b)　any other debts (not trade debts); and

(c)　the balance available between the invoiced debt and the amount lent by the factor; and

(d)　any sums which the factoring company owes to its client company because this will be a book debt under the bank's debenture.

6.13.4　Security interests

If another bank advancing further monies to the company, approaches your bank which has a floating charge, and requests your bank to waive its security rights in its favour, the bank can, instead of a waiver, give a certificate of non-crystallisation. This states that to the best of its knowledge it is not aware of any event that has caused the charge to crystallise.

If the bank gives a waiver, unless it is under a seal, it can be revoked by giving a reasonable notice, or if the party to whom it is given has not relied on it.

In case the bank later assigns the debt and security to another bank, the assignment and security to this other bank will be subject to the existing waiver.

6.13.5　Second charges created by the company

Where a bank holding a debenture as a security receives a notice of a second charge created by a company, the account must be stopped to preserve its priority.

6.13.6 Lien

A bank will not have any rights independent of an equitable mortgage, where the company deposits deeds or documents with the bank on an understanding that they will be returned to him when he performs his obligations or repays the bank. However, if the deeds deposited are supported by a written contract signed by the company, and the bank then creates a charge and registers it at the Companies Registry within 21 days of the deposit, it will be valid: *Re Molton Finance Ltd* [1967]; *Re Wallis and Simmonds (Builders) Ltd* [1975].

6.13.7 Book debts

A charge over book debts must be registered at Companies Registry within the required limit. Book debts constitute the company's property, but a charge over them gives the lender priority over ordinary creditors to recover debts due from the company: *Re Kent and Sussex Saw Mills Ltd* [1947].

6.14 CANCELLATION OF A REGISTERED CHARGE

Once the company has repaid the debt, the company may send to the registrar a Memorandum of Charge Ceasing to affect the company's property (form 403a), executed by the company and signed by a director and secretary on the reverse of the form, confirming the particulars stated to be correct.

The company is not obliged to file such a Memorandum of Charge Ceasing when the charge is discharged.

Once a charge on land is discharged, return the title documents to the company unless the bank has received a notice of a second mortgage, in which case the documents should be sent to the second mortgagee.

7 Insolvency and companies

Sections cited in this chapter refer to the Insolvency Act 1986 (IA 1986), unless otherwise stated.

When a company has financial problems and becomes unable to pay its debts as they fall due (s.123), the company may take the following steps:

1. A company may enter into a 'voluntary' arrangement with its creditors.
2. A secured creditor may appoint a receiver, usually under a floating charge (in this case known as an administrative receiver).
3. The court may make an administration order.
4. The company may go into liquidation.

7.1 ENTERING INTO VOLUNTARY ARRANGEMENT

This is a legally effective arrangement, which a company enters into with its creditors, for a part payment (composition) in satisfaction of its debts or a scheme of arrangement of its affairs (s.1(1)).

Voluntary arrangement may be proposed by either:

(a) the directors, provided the company is not subject to an administration order or in liquidation; or
(b) the liquidator or the administrator.

In either case the insolvency practitioner, called the 'nominee' at this stage, acts in relation to the voluntary arrangement for the purpose of supervision (but under (a) the company is not formally in liquidation). Separate meetings of members and creditors are arranged by the nominee who sets out his proposals of voluntary arrangement (s.3). If each of the meetings approves the voluntary arrangement, the arrangement is binding on the company and on all creditors (s.5).

7.1.1 Decisions of meetings

Proposals or modifications which affect the rights of a secured creditor cannot be approved at a meeting, without the creditor's express consent (s. 4(3)).

A preferential creditor's position is protected by s. 4(4), which provides that an arrangement which affects his rights to rank ahead of any non-preferential creditor for receipt of payment, and in proportion equal to that received by other preferential creditors, cannot be approved without his consent.

Objections to the scheme may be raised before the court by any creditor or member of the company, if they can show that either the interests of a creditor, member or contributory has been 'unfairly prejudiced' (s. 6(i)(a)); or there has been some material irregularity at one or any of the meetings (s. 6(1)(b)). If such an objection is upheld by the court, it may revoke or suspend the arrangement or may ask for revised proposals to be submitted for approval at a further meeting. The court may make an order to terminate or suspend the proceedings in cases where the company is in liquidation or is subject to an administration order.

The arrangement will be implemented by an insolvency practitioner, who is now called 'a supervisor'. He may not necessarily be the same practitioner who was the 'nominee' in the earlier stages.

Once a supervisor acts in the implementation of the arrangement, the company's bank must ensure that all transactions which pass through the company's bank account are authorised by him.

7.2   APPOINTMENT OF A RECEIVER

In this chapter, except where the context otherwise requires:

(a)   Any reference in the Companies Act or Insolvency Act to a receiver or manager of the property of a company, or to a receiver of it, includes a receiver or manager, or a receiver of part only of that property and a receiver only of the income arising from the property or from part of it; e.g. receivers appointed under s.101 of the Law of Property Act 1925 (LPA 1925).

(b)   In this chapter 'administrative receiver' means:
    (i)   a receiver or manager of the whole (or substantially the whole) of a company's property appointed by or on behalf of the holders of any debentures of the company secured by a charge which, as created, was a floating charge, or by such a charge and one or more securities; or
    (ii)   a person who would be such a receiver or manager but for the appointment of some other person as the receiver of part of the company's property.

A receiver, once appointed may take possession of the charged assets, sell them or obtain a court order for foreclosure. A receiver also takes control of the business in cases where a security of a floating charge over all its assets and undertaking is held. In this case he will be known as an administrative receiver. He will be a 'receiver and manager' if he takes control of the entire business. In the following paragraphs 'receiver' means a receiver of this type unless otherwise stated.

The receiver is usually appointed by the creditors (secured) under the terms of its debenture by which the charge was created. Unless he is appointed by the bank itself, the bank does not have to register the charge under which he is appointed. The receiver must accept his appointment within the following business day, otherwise his appointment will not be effective (s. 33). If the receiver's appointment is invalid, the court may order the person who made the appointment to indemnify him (s. 34).

If a bank holding a floating charge wishes to appoint an administrative receiver, it can only do so before an administration order is made.

Banks usually accept security of a debenture from limited companies, creating a fixed charge over specified fixed assets and all its 'assets and undertakings' by way of floating charge. The bank, upon the company's default, will enforce its security.

A secured creditor can appoint a receiver under the terms of the debenture creating the charge. Since an overdraft is repayable on demand (unless otherwise stated: *Williams & Glyn's Bank Ltd* v *Barnes* [1981]), the debtor must pay when demand for repayment is made. The bank owes no duty of care to the company in exercising its discretion whether or not to appoint a receiver, and is not obliged to take into consideration whether the company could refinance a loan before making demand for repayment and appointing a receiver: *Shamji & Others* v *Johnson Matthey Bankers Ltd & Others* [1986].

A receiver must not be a corporate body but an individual (s. 30). Unless specifically appointed by the court (s. 31), an undischarged bankrupt or a person disqualified by court order under s. 1 of the Company Directors Disqualification Act 1986 may be prevented from acting as a receiver, administrator or a liquidator.

It is important that a debenture holder appointing a receiver checks the powers given to the receiver by the debenture to ensure there are no restrictions in the debenture conflicting with the statutory powers.

If a fixed charge on the company's undertaking was given, the receiver will not be an administrative receiver and will control the assets subject to the charge under the powers given by the Law of Property Act to a receiver.

In *Meadrealm Ltd* v *Transcontinental Golf Construction Ltd* [1992], it was held that because the receiver was not appointed under the floating charge, he was not an administrative receiver.

7.2.1 Statutory duties on appointment of a receiver

A lender will appoint an LPA receiver under specific powers in the lender's mortgage and/or s.101 of LPA 1925.

Upon the LPA receiver's appointment:

(a)   The lender appointing a receiver must file his appointment with the Companies Registry in the prescribed form within seven days (s. 405, CA 1985).

(b)   Every business letter, invoice or order for goods issued on behalf of the company must contain a statement to the effect that a receiver has been appointed; i.e. 'Law of Property Act receiver appointed on (date)' (s.39).

(c)   Upon appointment, a receiver must advise the company and put a notice in the *London Gazette* (s. 46) (usually the company name will follow with the words 'in receivership').

(d)   The appointment must be in accordance with provisions of s. 33, IA 1986 and Rule 3.1 of the Insolvency Rules 1986.

(e)   Unless otherwise directed by the court, notice must be given to all the creditors within 28 days (s. 46), to the borrower (although it is not a strict requirement in a 'fixed charge' situation, it is advisable), and to all persons likely to be affected by the appointment, for example, guarantors.

(f)   The receiver must file accounts and returns of receipts and payments one month after the expiration of the first 12 months of the receiver's appointment, and thereafter one month after the expiration of every six months (s. 38(1), IA 1986).

7.2.2   Other duties of a receiver

Some of the duties of the receiver appointed under LPA 1925 have already been discussed in Chapter 5.

(a)   If the bank, as a secured creditor, has appointed the receiver, it should not interfere in the receiver's duties. Although by law, the receiver is an agent of the company, such interference may also make him the agent of the bank, thus making him liable for his conduct: *Standard Chartered Bank* v *Walker and Walker* (1982).

(b)   The receiver is under no duty to improve the property before selling it, but can decide to improve with a view to obtain better sale proceeds. In doing so the receiver should not act outside the scope of his powers without obtaining from the bank an 'indemnity' or 'comfort'. The decision in *Palk and Another* v *Mortgage Services Funding plc* [1993], challenged the view that the lender or receiver could hold back a sale for as long as they wanted.

In *American Express International Banking Corporation* v *Hurley* [1985], a receiver was subject to criticism for selling specialist and lighting equipment without advertising and without seeking specialist advice.

The receiver must obtain the best price reasonably obtainable: *Cuckmere Brick Co. Ltd* v *Mutual Finance Ltd* [1971]. Failing this he may be liable to the borrower and the guarantors: *Standard Chartered Bank* v *Walker and Walker* [1982].

A receiver usually obtains concurrence of all the lenders before attempting to sell the property. In *Re White Rose Cottage* [1965] it was held that a receiver cannot convey property free of subsequent mortgages or charges affecting them.

But according to the decision of the Judicial Committee in *Downsview Nominees Ltd* v *First City Corporation Ltd* [1993], a receiver does not owe a general duty to act with reasonable care, and as regards trading by him, his only duty is to be honest.

An administrative receiver has a duty to the borrower (the company) and to the person who has appointed him. He is entitled to dispose of assets without consulting the directors and withhold information which may affect the secured creditor: *Gomba Holdings UK Ltd* v *Homan* [1986].

In *Choudhri* v *Palta* [1992], it was held that where a court appoints a receiver over property which is already subject to charges in favour of banks, there was no power to grant receiver's costs and charges in priority to the banks' charges. It further stated that the court had power to order the administrative receiver to make good the deficiency and utilise the monies for discharging the sums secured by the security, if the court considers that the net proceeds realised on sale are less than the net amount which would be realised in the open market by a willing vendor (s. 43(3)(b)). Even after a receiver is appointed, the directors still retain some powers (e.g. to hold a general meeting if the company has to be wound up), and may protect the rights of the company if the receiver fails to do so: *Watts* v *Midland Bank plc* [1986].

7.2.3 Steps to be taken by the lenders where the powers of the Law of Property Act receivers are inadequate

If a lender has only a fixed charge as security over land, and it is important for realisation purposes that the business is continued on a going concern basis, a lender can overcome this difficulty as follows:

(a) if the borrower is agreeable, ask him to transfer the business and remaining non-charged assets into a new company, which can then continue the business until it is sold; or

(b) if the borrower does not co-operate, the receiver (provided the security gives him power) can appoint a manager to run a business. Under this method, a receiver will neither be able to monitor the assets nor run the business under a fixed charge.

7.2.4 Action to be taken by the bank when an administrative receiver is appointed

1. As soon as a receiver is appointed, he assumes control of the assets and responsibilities of the directors and may be expected to advise the bank of the appointment.

2. The bank should obtain a preliminary report from the administrative receiver after the appointment (usually within 14 days).

3. The directors' authority to draw cheques on the company's account will cease upon the receiver's appointment, and the bank should not pay the cheques (unless authorised by the receiver) returning them with answer 'refer to drawer, receiver appointed'.

4. An administrative receiver will open an administrative receiver's account at the bank where the company account is held. Most administrative receivers operate separate accounts for fixed and floating charge realisations.

When the account in the name of a receiver is opened, the bank should have sight of the debenture by which he has been appointed and obtain his specimen signature. Designate the company account appropriately; e.g. 'A Ltd, B Administrative Receiver'.

5. Subject to the rules of statutory set off, a bank may set off the company's liability to the bank against a credit balance held on the company's account. If the company maintains several accounts, some of which are in credit and the others in debit, apply the credit balances on a pro rata basis to the debit balances. Do not apply credit balances to a non-preferential account, so as to maximise a preferential claim: *Re Unit 2 Windows Ltd* [1985].

6. Check the legal mortgage to ensure that the powers given to the receiver are wide enough to carry out the anticipated job. Usually a receiver appointed under a mortgage will have conferred on him only the statutory powers under LPA 1925, but a well worded mortgage may give him extended powers. When the company goes into liquidation (or an individual becomes bankrupt) the agency ceases, but the receiver can continue to act under 'Barrows' powers: *Barrows* v *The Chief Land Registrar* [1977].

7.2.5 Borrowing by the receiver

Examine the debenture to ensure that the receiver's statutory power is not affected by any restrictions or conditions imposed on the receiver's borrowing (s. 42 (1)).

Unless and until the company goes into liquidation, the receiver is by law deemed to be an agent of the company (s. 44(1)(a)) and is personally liable on any contracts which he enters into whilst carrying out his functions (s. 44(1)(b)). But the receiver is entitled to be indemnified out of company assets against these liabilities (s. 44(1)(c)).

The bank will have priority over other ordinary creditors in cases where a bank would by subrogation be entitled to have the rights of the receiver against the company assets if the receiver fails to meet his obligations to the bank.

If the administrative receiver needs to borrow for trading purposes to continue business as a 'going concern', or requires short term facilities to complete profitable contracts, provided the receiver has accepted full personal liability and the bank is agreeable to lend for these purposes, the administrative receiver's written confirmation on the standard facility letter, detailing the facility and the arrangement fees, must be obtained.

Before agreeing to advance monies to the administrative receiver, enquire from him/her:

(a)   the source from which the advance will be repaid. If the company's assets are less than its liabilities, they may not even be sufficient to pay the receiver's fees, in which case, any further monies lent by the bank may not be recoverable.

(b)   if the receiver can provide any security in respect of the advance and if so, whether the bank will have priority over the existing charge under which he is appointed. If the receiver agrees to this, the bank should enter into a deed of priority with the secured creditor.

An administrative receiver can terminate the appointment by first placing the company into liquidation to conclude the company's affairs properly and then by filing a Notice of Ceasing to Act at the Companies Registration office. In the event of an administrative receiver's death during the course of holding office, the bank should inform the Registrar of Companies on form 37, and the company or its liquidator, and the members of the creditors' committee (if any), if the company is in liquidation (Rule 3.34).

7.3 ADMINISTRATION ORDERS

An administration order may be made by a court, whereby it will appoint an insolvency practitioner to act as an administrator of the company with similar powers to those vested in a receiver under Schedule 1 of the Act. 'The administrator' is a person appointed by the court under an administration order for the purpose of managing the affairs, business and property of the company during the period for which the order is in force.

A receiver only has certain specific duties to an unsecured creditor, but he does not represent unsecured creditors' interest. These unsecured creditors have no power to appoint a receiver and they may not be able to protect their interests as they have no control over a receiver appointed by a secured creditor. Under the provisions of Part II of IA 1986, instead of appointing a receiver, the company, its directors or its creditors may petition to the court to make an 'administration order'. In *Re A Company* [1986], it was held that pending hearing of the petition and in the time between service and hearing of the petition, under s. 9, the court had power to appoint a manager over the company's business and assets.

A bank, with a security of a floating charge, may not have yet appointed an administrative receiver or contemplate doing so, but if the court advises the floating charge holder bank of a petition for an administration order (s.9(2)) the floating charge holder bank can, within five days, appoint an administrative receiver with instructions to refuse the administration order (s.9(3)(a)). Usually a debenture has an event of default clause empowering it to appoint an administrative receiver.

In *Re Croftbell Ltd* [1990], an attempt by a company to stop a bank from appointing an administrator did not succeed.

The court may make an administration order if it is satisfied that it will achieve one or more of the following purposes (s.8(3)):

(a) the survival of the company and either the whole or any part of its undertaking as a going concern; or

(b) to lead to the approval by creditors in due course of a voluntary arrangement; or

(c) the company and its creditors or members under the provisions of CA 1985, s.425, may reach a compromise or a scheme of arrangement in time; or

(d) a more advantageous realisation of the company's assets than would be effected in a winding up (s. 8 (3)).

A court has a discretion in relation to the full procedural timetable set out in the Insolvency Rules: *Re Cavco Floors Ltd* [1990].

In *Re Land and Property Trust Company plc* [1991], a petition for an administration order was rejected as there was no evidence that the voluntary arrangement would be acceptable to the creditors, and because it was not likely that the statutory purpose would be achieved. In *Re SCL Building Services Ltd* [1989], the same view was held.

During the period between the date of presentation of a petition for an administrative order and the date of making of an order or the dismissal of the petition, a moratorium on any of the following action is imposed by s. 10:

(a)   no resolution for voluntary winding up and an order for compulsory liquidation, but a petition for winding up may be presented;

(b)   no proceedings may be commenced for seizure of the company's goods in execution of a judgment debt without leave of the court;

(c)   no steps may be taken for repossession of goods from the company which are subject to any hire purchase agreement, conditional sale agreement or retention of title agreement without leave of the court; or for the commencement of continuance of legal proceedings against the company without the leave of the court (s. 10).

Within three months (or longer if permitted by the court) of the appointment, an administrator must convene a meeting of creditors and present for their approval proposals for dealing with the task for which he was appointed. The creditors' meeting may accept or modify the administrator's proposals (with his consent). The administrator will have to report the outcome of the meeting to the court.

If the creditors' meeting rejects the proposals, the court may order for the compulsory liquidation of the company or make whatever further order it considers necessary.

Any creditor or member of the company may report and complain about the administrator's conduct to the court, seeking a relief against his unfair prejudicial action to some or all the creditors or members, including himself (s. 27) (*Re Charnley Davies Ltd* [1990]).

Under rule 7.47 of the Insolvency Rules 1986, on a creditor's application, the court may rescind any order which it had made.

In *Cornhill Finance Services Ltd* v *Cornhill Insurance plc* [1992], an administration order was revoked at the instance of a creditor. Based on this decision the court may rescind applications for an administration order on the grounds of material non-disclosure and prejudice to the creditor who lodged an application under rule 7.47.

Before seeking administration orders, sufficient notice to appropriate parties must be given so as to enable them to be heard on the petition: *Re Rowbotham Baxter Ltd* [1990].

An administrative receiver acts in the interests of the creditor who has appointed him, whereas an administrator acts in the interests of all creditors.

A bank should calculate a preferential claim, although preferential creditors do not arise in administration, because if the company subsequently goes into liquidation, the 'relevant date' for the bank's preferential claim will date back to the date of the administration order.

7.3.1   Enforcing liens against administrators

Secured creditors cannot realise their security without the consent of the administrator or the leave of the court (s. 11(3)(c)).

In *Re Paramount Airways Ltd* [1991] and *Re Atlantic Computer Systems plc* [1992], it was stated that it is not the purpose of s. 11(3) to convert a secured creditor into an unsecured creditor.

The danger of not complying with s. 11(3) was specified in the decision in *Re Sabre International Products Ltd* [1991], where it was held that, although the administrators have a duty to behave in a fair, reasonable manner, they do not have a duty to 'hold the hand of a security holder'.

7.3.2   Powers of an administrator (s. 14)

Steps to be followed when an administrator is appointed:

If the bank has not appointed an administrative receiver because it does not have a security of a floating charge it will only become aware of the administration order when made and in respect of voting at the creditors' meeting it will rank as an unsecured creditor even if the loan it has given is fully secured.

It should be noted that an administrator owes no duty to the secured creditors.

Appointment of an administrator is beneficial where there are many foreign assets and the retention of title clauses do not apply.

An administrator may:

(a)   appoint any person to be a director of a company or remove them from office;

(b)   challenge past transactions of the company and have them reversed by court order;

(c)   deal with assets that are subject to a floating charge as if that charge did not exist; although the secured creditor retains rights over whatever replaces the assets (normally cash).

(d)   With the consent of the court or approval of the charge holder, the administrator may sell the property of the company which is subject to a fixed charge (s. 11). An administrator should consult the shareholders even if there is no likelihood of recovering any proceeds: *Re Consumer and Industrial Press Ltd* [1988]. An administrator may sell the property subject to a floating charge, in which case the charge will then be transferred to the proceeds of sale: (s. 15).

(e)   Without the consent of an administrator or a court, a supplier of goods, etc., on hire purchase or retention of title conditions, cannot repossess the goods (s. 11(3)).

(f)   All business letters, invoices, and orders for goods must show the administrator's name, and indicate that the company is subject to an administration order (s. 12).

7.3.3   Action to be taken by the bank

In respect of security
When an administrator has been appointed, where the bank is fully secured by direct security, provide details of the account, as at the date of the order, and of the security.
    If the bank does not have a direct security or is not fully secured, it should consider if it wants to participate in voting at the creditors' meeting.

(a)   Creditors with security
A creditor with the power to appoint a receiver over specific company assets may not do so once a petition for an administration order has been presented. But with the power to appoint an administrative receiver over most or all of a company's assets, he may do so at any time before an administration order is made. If one is appointed, an administration order will not normally be made.
    Goods supplied by a creditor, under a retention of title, hire purchase, conditional sale or chattel leasing agreement cannot be repossessed after a

167

petition has been presented, but an administrator cannot dispose of them without the consent of either the creditor or the court.

A creditor whose security includes retention of title, or hire purchase agreement etc., is entitled to vote at meetings only for any unsecured part of its debt.

(b)   Unsecured creditors

Once a petition for an administration order has been presented to the court, no action can be taken to recover outstanding debts.

The administrator may continue or terminate existing contracts.

Contracts and commitments entered into by the administrator will be paid out of the available assets.

The administrator must send notice of an administration order to creditors within 28 days.

The administrator must send, to the creditors, a copy of the proposals and notice of a creditors' meeting to be held no later than three months after his appointment and before he puts any of the proposals into effect.

Creditors entitled to vote at the creditors' meeting can vote for or against the proposals, and can suggest amendments. Voting is by simple majority.

Creditors are entitled to VAT bad debt relief, if there would be no dividend in a liquidation.

7.3.4   Opening an account

(a)   When the administrator wants to open an account, obtain a copy of the court order appointing him and designate the account specifying his status; e.g. 'Carl Parker, Administrator of Healey Ltd'.

An administrator, like an administrative receiver, performs all his actions in exercise of his official powers as the company's agent (s. 14), but there is no statutory provision making him personally liable on contracts.

A third party (the bank) dealing with the administrator in good faith and for value is entitled to assume that he is acting in good faith (s. 14(6)).

(b)   If the bank, which does not have a security of a floating charge, is owed money by a debtor against whom petition is presented, it will not become aware of the proceedings until after the order is made. In respect of voting at the creditors' meeting, it will rank as an unsecured creditor to the extent of its unsecured debt even if the loan it has given is fully secured. An administrator owes no duty to the secured creditors. Appointment of an administrator is beneficial where there are many foreign assets and the retention of title clauses do not apply.

7.4 WINDING UP (OR LIQUIDATION)

A company can be put into liquidation voluntarily or compulsorily. In either case, a liquidator is appointed so that the company can be dissolved.

(a) In a compulsory liquidation the company is put into liquidation by order of the court.

(b) In a voluntary liquidation a resolution is passed at a general meeting, by three-quarters majority of votes cast.

There are two types of voluntary liquidation:

(a) members' voluntary liquidation – where the company is solvent and can pay all its creditors in full. The directors make a statutory declaration of solvency; and

(b) creditors' voluntary liquidation – here the company is insolvent and cannot pay its creditors in full. In this case the company must call a meeting of creditors giving at least seven days' notice.

7.5 COMPULSORY LIQUIDATION

When a petition is presented to the court requesting a winding up order to be made due to the company's inability to pay its debts (as defined in s. 123) and the court issues a winding up order, it is called compulsory liquidation.

A petition can be presented by a creditor who can show that a company owes him more than £750 (ss. 122–123); or by a shareholder, provided the company is insolvent, or by the whole board of directors: *Re Instrumentation Electrical Services Ltd* [1989]. All the directors' powers cease when a winding up order is made: *Fowler v Broad's Patent Night Light Co.* [1893].

Presentation of petition to the court is advertised in the *London Gazette*.

The petition will be made on the following grounds:

(a) The creditor has issued a statutory demand for payment and the company has failed to pay the sums due or offer security within three weeks. If the debt is being disputed, the court will not make a winding up order: *Re London and Paris Banking Corporation* [1874]; or

(b) The creditor has obtained judgment against the company and has not been successful in executing the judgment, as it is returned unsatisfied in whole or in part; or

169

(c)   The company is unable to pay its debts as they fall due: *Re Patrick and Lyon Ltd* [1933]; *Re Capital Annuities Ltd* [1978]; *Re Wm. C. Leitch Brothers Ltd* [1932].

The grounds on which the company may be wound up by the court are:

(i)   The company has passed a special resolution to that effect.
(ii)   The company is unable to pay its debts.
(iii) The number of members is reduced below two.
(iv)   The company does not commence business within a year of incorporation, or suspends its business for a year.
(v)   If the company is an old public company, under s. 1 of the Companies Consolidation (Consequential Provisions) Act 1985.
(vi)   If the company has been registered as a public company for more than a year since incorporation, but has not been issued with a certificate under s. 117 of the Companies Act 1985.
(vii) The court is of the opinion that it is just and equitable to wind up the company.

7.5.1   Consequences of the order for compulsory liquidation (ss. 127 and 128)

Upon the making of a compulsory order:

(a)   Any disposition of the company's property or transfer of shares made after the presentation of petition is void unless otherwise ordered by the court (s. 127).
(b)   Executions or attachments levied subsequently are void.
(c)   The court's permission is required if any action against the company is to proceed.
(d)   The directors' powers cease.

The company in these circumstances may:

(a)   lodge an application to the court for the appointment of a provisional liquidator, so that he can take charge of the company's assets pending the hearing of the petition (s. 135);

(b)   obtain an anticipatory validation order under s. 127, allowing the company to carry on its business and make drawings on its bank account until the hearing of the petition;

(c)   carry on the business in anticipation that the court will not make order for compulsory liquidation, and if it does, then convince the court to approve the company's transactions since the date of the petition under s.127.

7.5.2   Bank procedures pending the hearing of the petition

A bank is under a duty to check the *Gazette* to see if any winding up petitions against a customer company are made: *Re McGuinness Brothers (UK) Ltd* [1987].

Upon hearing of a petition for compulsory winding up, the company's existing account must be stopped. Return the cheques, 'refer to drawer: petition for winding up presented'. The bank will not be able to claim protection of s. 127 if any disposition of the property, or future operation of the account after the date of the petition, is made without the order of the court: *Re Grays Inn Construction Co. Ltd* [1980].

The court may exercise its discretion for making an order to allow these transactions: *Re T. W. Construction Ltd* [1954], and may take into consideration:

(a)   the solvency of the company;

(b)   whether or not creditors are likely to be prejudiced: *Re A Company* [1986]. The court will try to balance the claims of unsecured creditors and those claiming under the disposition: *Re Tramway Building and Construction Co. Ltd* [1988];

(c)   if the company can prove that carrying on of the business is for the purpose of avoiding a loss: *Re Operator Control Cabs* [1970];

(d)   if the company intends to sell assets in order to avoid losing them because of a liquidation order: *Re A. I. Levy Holdings Ltd* [1964].

If the court has granted an anticipatory Validation Order under s. 127, then the bank may allow the company to open a new account for the purpose of depositing cheques from its debtors and drawing the monies upon the clearance of the cheques: *D B Evans (Bilston) Ltd* v *Barclays Bank Ltd* [1961].

The provisional liquidator, upon his appointment, will advise the bank of the appointment.

7.5.3 Bank procedures after order for compulsory liquidation

1. After the court makes an order for compulsory liquidation, the official receiver will be notified and become the liquidator.

2. Copies of the notice will be sent by the official receiver, to the company and to the Companies Registry, which will in turn give notice of the order in the *London Gazette*.

3. Within 12 weeks from the making of the order, the official receiver may obtain a formal 'statement of affairs' from the directors or others connected with the company. He may hold a separate meeting of the creditors and members.

The official receiver may apply to the Companies Registry for the dissolution of the company, if he believes that the assets are not sufficient to cover liquidation expenses, and no further investigation is necessary.

4. After the order is made, the bank should stop all the accounts and open a new account in the company's name, in accordance with the procedures outlined in section 7.7, which are applicable to both voluntary and compulsory winding up.

5. Set off credit and debit balances if mutuality under Rule 4.90 of IA1986 exists.

7.6 VOLUNTARY LIQUIDATION

7.6.1 Members' voluntary liquidation

The directors give 21 days notice to hold a general meeting to pass a special resolution to wind up the company and appoint a liquidator. It will require approval of a three-quarters' majority of votes cast.

The directors file a statutory declaration of solvency at Companies Registry, if they are certain that the company for which the petition has been presented will be able to pay its debts in full within12 months.

If the company is then not able to pay its debts in full within 12 months, the directors have to pay criminal penalties unless they can justify that the declaration was made on reasonable grounds (s. 89). The liquidation will then proceed as a creditors' voluntary winding up (s. 96).

Notice of the resolution and an appointment naming the liquidator will be advertised in the *London Gazette*.

On assuming office, the liquidator will give notice of his appointment to the bank. Unless otherwise decided at the general meeting or by the liquidator, the power of all the directors will cease (s. 91(2)).

After receipt of notice of appointment of the liquidator, the bank will return all cheques marked 'refer to drawer: winding up resolution passed'. The liquidator will open an account for the company in his own name.

7.6.2 Creditors' voluntary liquidation

If the company is insolvent and passes an extraordinary resolution (by three-quarters' majority of votes cast) that it cannot, on the basis of its liabilities, carry on its business, it is called a voluntary winding up (s. 84(1)(c)).

A notice of the meeting of creditors is advertised in the *London Gazette* (s. 85(1)).

Voluntary winding up commences on the day of the passing of the resolution (s. 86). From this date, the company will only carry on business for the purpose of its beneficial winding up (s. 87(1)).

The meeting nominates a liquidator (who must be an insolvency practitioner) and creditors (not less than three nor more than five) to serve on the committee of inspection.

If the creditors believe that they are unlikely to be paid in full the sums owed to them, they may nominate their own liquidator, failing which the company may do so (s. 100(1)).

If the creditors do not appoint a liquidator, the office will be taken by the members' nominee. However, even if a liquidator is appointed by them, they will actually appoint him at the meeting which takes place in two weeks' time. In this interim period of two weeks, the members' nominee will act as a liquidator. In the past the presence of the members' nominee has been exploited for the purpose known as 'centrebinding': *Re Centrebind Ltd* [1966].

To protect and prevent the disposal of the company's assets at an undervalue before the actual appointment of a liquidator, the powers vested in the members' nominee as liquidator are restricted under s. 166 to:

(a) take control of all the property belonging to the company;

(b) dispose of perishable and other goods which might reduce their value if not immediately disposed of; and

(c) do all things necessary for the protection of the company's assets.

Leave of the court will be required if the members' nominee wishes to carry out any other act than those mentioned above.

The notice of the creditors' meeting will be sent to the debtor company's bank. Upon receipt of the notice, the security charged must be valued. If the debt exceeds the value of the security, the bank may only vote at the meeting as an unsecured creditor in respect of the excess debt over the security.

7.7 BANK PROCEDURE FOR VOLUNTARY AND COMPULSORY WINDING UP

1. Open a new account in the company's name in accordance with the liquidator's mandate and instructions.
2. Only honour cheques signed by the liquidator or by authorised persons named in the mandate.
3. Ask for the evidence of the licence under which the liquidator is appointed. If appointed as the members' and not the creditors' nominee, then the bank should require evidence that the creditors' meeting has been duly convened and held.
4. The credit balance on one account in the company's name may be set off against the outstanding debt to the bank on another, provided mutuality exists between the two accounts (in accordance with Insolvency Rule 4.90) and provided it is not a trust account (*Re Unit 2 Windows* rule should also be borne in mind).
5. Advise the outstanding balances on the account to the liquidator.

In case of a compulsory liquidation, the liquidator will pay all monies received by him into the Insolvency Services Account at the Bank of England, unless the liquidation company has DTI approval for the liquidator to have a local bank account, in which case ask for written consent from the DTI before opening the account. Follow the same procedure if a 'special manager' is appointed.

7.8 LIQUIDATOR'S BORROWINGS

The liquidator, who needs to borrow money and give security for the purpose of continuing the company's business with a view to selling it as a going concern, does not have to obtain a sanction. In respect of borrowings in large sums, a sanction of the liquidation committee or, in a members' voluntary liquidation, of the members in general meeting is usually required.

Before lending the monies the bank should be satisfied that the loan is for the purpose of carrying on the business for the company's beneficial winding up. In the case of a compulsory liquidation, the bank should ask for the evidence of a court order (s. 167(1)) authorising the liquidator to exercise his powers.

7.9 INSOLVENCY PRACTITIONER'S BANK ACCOUNT

Ask for the evidence of the insolvency practitioner's written appointment, either the court order in a compulsory liquidation; or a certified copy of the resolution of the general meeting, or of the creditors' meeting appointing him as a liquidator, in voluntary liquidation.

7.10   PRIORITY OF CHARGES AND EXPENSES OF AN INSOLVENT COMPANY

If the receiver is appointed under a floating charge, he must pay preferential debts first and then other secured debts. On the assumption that the company has given fixed and floating charge, the receiver will pay the debts in the following order:

(a)   Secured creditors up to the value of the assets charged. Any surplus, will be utilised to pay other secured debts. If there is a deficit, the remaining unpaid debt of secured creditors under their fixed charge will be treated as an unsecured debt.

The bank ranking as a secured creditor has the following options:
    (i)   rely on the security and do not prove it;
    (ii)   realise the security and prove for the loss, if any;
    (iii) value the security and prove for the loss, if any;
    (iv) release the security and prove for the entire debt (not usually followed by the banks).

The bank should credit the proceeds to a suspense account when third party security is realised.

(b)   Administrative costs and charges, and remuneration of the receiver. This ranks in priority to the creditors' debts, or if a liquidator is appointed in a compulsory winding up, by s.156, priority of his expenses are at the discretion of the court.

(c)   Preferential debts rank ahead of a floating charge holder's debt (s. 175). Preferential creditors in this category would include the following:
    (i)   Twelve months' deductions of PAYE prior to the relevant date.
    (ii)   VAT claims up to six months prior to the relevant date.
    (iii) Assessment of social security contributions (Class 1 and 2), 12 months before the relevant date and 12 months' assessment of Class 4, before 5 April prior to the relevant date.
    (iv) Contributions relating to State and Occupational Pension Scheme Contributions.
    (v)   Arrears of employees' wages or salary for up to four months, with a maximum limit of £800 per employee, prior to the relevant date.
    (vi) Accrued holiday remuneration.
    (vii) Any sums lent by the bank under (v) and (vi) above.

After realisation, if preferential claims are not satisfied in full, they are distributed proportionately.

The provisions as to what constitutes the 'relevant date' as regards a preferential claim as outlined in ss. 386 and 387 are:

   (i)   A voluntary winding up (members' or creditors') commences when the resolution to wind up the company is passed.

   (ii)   A compulsory winding up commences at the date the petition is presented to the court.

   (iii) When an administrative receiver is appointed.

   (iv) On appointment of an administrator, if subsequently, the company is wound up by the court.

Where a bank appoints an administrative receiver under the debenture it holds, the bank must ensure that the receiver has made provision for preferential creditors, otherwise both the receiver and the bank will be liable in damages to the preferential creditors: *I.R.C.* v *Goldblatt* [1972].

A bank may be able to appropriate proceeds under the terms of its mortgage: *Re William Hall (Contractors) Ltd* [1967].

If a winding up petition is presented within six months of taking security, the security may be void if the liquidator can prove that it was a preference.

7.11 THE EARLY WARNING PROCEDURE

If a bank finds the value of its security falls drastically or believes that a business or company is likely to file for bankruptcy or go into liquidation, it should open a separate wages and salaries account in the name of the business or company.

If a bank or a director of the company has lent monies to pay wages, salaries or holiday remuneration, it will, by virtue of subrogation, gain priority in respect of these preferentials for a maximum period of four months, limited to £800 per employee. Monies lent by employers to subcontractors will not be covered by virtue of subrogation: *Re C.W. and A.L. Hughes Ltd* [1966].

However, in the case of *Re Primrose (Builders) Ltd* [1950], it was held that it was not necessary to open a separate wages account to gain priority for preferential claim, although it is advisable to do so because it is easy to monitor and the rule in *Clayton's* case will not operate against the bank where the wages are paid from the running account and subsequent credits repay such debts for wages.

In *National Provincial Bank Ltd* v *Freedman and Rubens* [1934], the bank agreed to pay wages cheques on a condition that they were backed by credits. It was held that the bank was not appropriating payments, but monitoring the extent of the overdraft. Therefore operation of the account was subject to *Clayton's* case and a claim for wages advances was subject to its application.

In *Re Unit 2 Windows Ltd* [1985], it was held that where several credit and debit accounts of a business are held, in the event of liquidation, the credit balances should not only be applied to a non-preferential claim, but they must also be applied on a pro rata basis to the debit balances.

In *Re James R. Rutherford & Sons Ltd* [1964], the bank did not allow the wages and salaries account of a company to reach the four month maximum amount, because it inadvertently made transfers to the company's trading account each month commencing at the end of the first month. The bank successfully claimed that not only were the wages and salaries account preferential, but also the wages and salaries transferred to the trading account which had not been wiped out by the operation of *Clayton's* case up to the statutory limits.

7.12   FLOATING CHARGE HOLDER

1.   If the company is insolvent when the floating charge is created and it goes into liquidation within twelve months of creating the charge, the charge will only be effective in respect of new monies advanced: *Re Thomas Mortimer Ltd* [1925]. Any invalid claim will be treated as an unsecured claim.

2.   Preferential debts rank ahead of debts secured by floating charges, but because most banks' mortgage forms contain a clause allowing, in respect of certain assets (i.e. sale proceeds recovered from a voluntary sale by the company before winding up or receivership) to convert a floating charge into a fixed charge, they would have priority over preferential debts.

As regards priority agreement between charges, in *Re Portbase (Clothing) Ltd* [1993], a first chargee with a fixed charge on book debts agreed to postpone its charge and rank subsequent in priority after a later chargee holding a floating charge. The company had gone into liquidation after the crystallisation of a floating charge so that the payment to a floating charge holder was made before that to a fixed charge holder. The first chargee could have instead maintained its order of priority, but agreed to forward receipts to the later chargee.

3.   Under the provisions of ss. 115 and 175(2), in liquidation, payments for liquidation expenses are made in priority to payments to preferential creditors. Banks must therefore bear in mind that the floating charge assets will be subject to both these claims when liquidation occurs, whilst an administrative receivership is still in progress.

4.   Unsecured creditors, i.e. trade creditors, rank equally.

5.   The members of shareholders rank equally or according to the provisions in the articles.

PART II: MAJOR LEGAL CASES

1. Williams and Glyn's Bank Ltd v Boland [1981]

Mr Boland was the proprietor of the matrimonial home (registered title) which he mortgaged to the bank, without Mrs Boland's knowledge. The mortgage was to fund Mr Boland's business venture. Mrs Boland had contributed to the cost of the home. The previous home was in their joint names. Mrs Boland had not registered a caution at the Land Registry to protect her equitable interest in the property. When the bank took the mortgage from Mr Boland, it did not make any enquiries and was unaware of the circumstances on which Mrs Boland's interest was founded. The bank sought possession of the property when Mr Boland failed to repay the loan.

HELD: Mrs Boland had occupied the property and made contributions to its purchase and maintenance, thus gaining an overriding interest under s.70(1)(g) of the Land Registration Act 1925 which the purchaser could discover by inspection. The bank had failed to enquire whether the owner's wife was in occupation and if so, whether she had an equitable interest as a result of her contribution to the purchase price. The Court of Appeal and the House of Lords upheld Mrs Boland's interest.

2. Lloyds Bank Ltd v Bundy [1975]

Mr Bundy was a customer of the bank where his son's company also held an account. Mr Bundy executed a series of guarantees supported by a legal mortgage over his farm to secure liabilities of his son's company. In the past Mr Bundy had relied on the bank for financial advice. The bank knew that the company was in financial difficulties, but did not explain this fully to Mr Bundy, although it knew that he relied upon them for advice in such matters. The company went into receivership and the bank sought possession of the farm. Mr Bundy claimed that the guarantee and the mortgage were both obtained by undue influence and therefore he was not liable.

HELD: As the relationship between Mr Bundy and the bank was that of trust and confidence, which imposed a duty on the bank to insist that he received independent legal advice before executing the security, the bank failed in that duty. The guarantee and mortgage were therefore set aside on the grounds of undue influence.

3. National Westminster Bank plc v Morgan [1985]

Mr and Mrs Morgan were joint owners of their family home. They mortgaged

179

it to the bank to secure the refinancing of a previous loan from the Abbey National Building Society, on which they fell into arrears when Mr Morgan's business got into difficulties. Mrs Morgan did not want the new mortgage to extend to advances for her husband's business activities and she was assured, wrongly but in good faith, by the bank manager that it did not. The bank sought possession of the house when the loan repayments were in arrears. Mr Morgan died soon afterwards without any business debts to the bank and Mrs Morgan appealed against a possession order on the grounds that she had signed the legal charge because of undue influence from the bank manager.

HELD: The appeal was dismissed and the possession order upheld by the House of Lords. Mrs Morgan had not suffered manifest disadvantage by signing the mortgage because it had enabled her to remain in her home. Nor had the bank exploited its position. On the facts there was no confidential or fiduciary relationship between the bank and Mrs Morgan.

4. *Avon Finance Co. Ltd* v *Bridger* [1985]
Mr and Mrs Bridger purchased a retirement home partly with a mortgage and partly from a contribution made by their son. They were not aware that the sum he contributed was raised through a loan from Avon Finance against the security of a second charge on the property. The son, by misleading them as to its nature and by exerting undue influence over them, had persuaded his parents to execute the charge at the office of Avon Finance's solicitor. Avon Finance sought possession of the house when the son defaulted on the loan.

HELD: A possession order was declined because Avon Finance had used the son as its agent to obtain the Bridgers' signatures on the charge, and as a result of the transaction the Bridger's had also suffered a real disadvantage. This decision was approved by the House of Lords in *Barclays Bank plc* v *O'Brien* [1993].

5. *Bank of Credit and Commerce International SA* v *Aboody* [1989]
Mrs Aboody purchased a matrimonial home in her sole name, and Mr Aboody persuaded her to mortgage it to secure a loan to a company controlled by him, of which Mrs Aboody was a director. In fact Mrs Aboody never took an active part in the company's business affairs and signed any document her husband put in front of her. BCCI sought a possession order when the company defaulted on the loan.

HELD: The order was granted. Although Mrs Aboody had acted under her husband's dominance and he in turn was acting as agent for the bank, Mrs Aboody had not suffered manifest disadvantage at the time she signed the documents, but had benefited from the support the loan had given to the company's business.

In both Avon Finance and Aboody the person exercising undue influence was held to be acting as an agent of the mortgagee.

6. *Coldunell Ltd* v *Gallon* [1986]

Here a money lender, Coldunell, advanced short term business finance to the son of the Gallons (elderly parents) on security of a mortgage on their home executed by Mr Gallon. The mortgaged property was registered in the name of Mr Gallon and Mrs Gallon had consented to the mortgage. Coldunell's solicitor prepared the necessary documents for execution by the Gallons and intended to post them to the Gallons together with a letter advising them to seek independent legal advice before signing. The son intercepted the letters, withheld the solicitor's advice from his parents and persuaded them to sign the charge and the consent respectively. When the son defaulted on repayments Coldunell sought a possession order against the Gallons.

HELD: The court refused to set aside the mortgage although the Gallons had clearly signed the documents under the influence of their son and had suffered manifest disadvantage as a result, because their son was not an agent of the money lender, the possession order was therefore granted. The court refused to set aside the mortgage because the undue influence was that of a third party and not the mortgagee.

7. *Kingsnorth Trust Ltd* v *Bell* [1986]

The husband, Mr Bell wished to borrow money to buy a business property for which he required his wife's consent to a charge on the matrimonial home in which she had an overriding interest. Kingsnorth Trust's solicitor sent Bell's solicitor the necessary documents which the latter gave to Bell for signature by himself and his wife. Mr Bell misled his wife as to the purpose of the advance and by fraudulent misrepresentation procured her consent for a charge on the matrimonial home in which she had an overriding interest.

HELD: Mr Bell was acting as Kingsnorth Trust's sub-agent, thus preventing Kingsnorth Trust from obtaining a possession order upon Mr Bell's default. The charge was voidable for undue influence.

8. *Lloyds Bank plc v Waterhouse* **[1991]**

A father guaranteed a loan to his son from the bank to enable his son to buy a farm. The bank also took a charge over the farm. The guarantee was in the bank's standard form and contained an 'all monies' clause securing all his son's indebtedness to the bank in respect of any other borrowing the son might make. The father did not read the guarantee because he was illiterate, but he did enquire of the bank the terms of the guarantee. The father was called upon to pay under his guarantee when the son defaulted.

HELD: The father had questioned the bank and was therefore not careless. Because the bank had negligently misrepresented the terms of the guarantee, he was not liable.

9. *Lloyds Bank plc v Rossett* **[1990]**

Mr Rossett purchased a house in his sole name and with his own money. Mrs Rossett did not live at the property, but undertook and performed decorating work. Major renovations were carried out by the builders. Mr Rossett borrowed from the bank against the security of the property without Mrs Rossett's knowledge. The bank sought a possession order when Mr Rossett defaulted. Mrs Rossett defended the claim, arguing that she had an overriding interest.

HELD: Mrs Rossett had not made sufficient contribution to establish an equitable interest in the house.

In *Midland Bank Ltd v Dobson* [1985], although the wife had contributed towards the upkeep and costs of decoration of the property, which was purchased by her husband and her mother in law, but was registered in the sole name of her husband, she could not protect her right of occupation of the property as an overriding interest.

10. *Abbey National Building Society v Cann* **[1990]**

The house was purchased with a joint contribution, partly from the mortgagor, partly by the purchaser and partly by the third party (the purchaser's mother). The mortgagor was not aware of the third party's beneficial interest. The mother was abroad and not in actual occupation when the building society advanced mortgage monies to the purchaser's (son's) solicitor before the completion date.

HELD: The purchaser's mother was not in actual occupation at the time of creation of charge or transfer of land. Thus the mortgagee had an equitable charge over the property and priority over the mother's beneficial interest.

11. *Standard Chartered Bank* v *Walker and Walker* **[1982]**
The guarantors had guaranteed their company's borrowing. When the company defaulted, the bank appointed a receiver under its debenture and instructed him to arrange for a quick sale by auction of the company's machinery. As the sale was poorly advertised and held during extremely bad weather, receipts from the sale amounted to less than half the estimate.

HELD: The bank was liable to both the company (the debtor) and the guarantor for the shortfall, because it had interfered with the receivership.

12. *Cuckmere Brick Co. Ltd* v *Mutual Finance Ltd* **[1971]**
In exercising their power of sale, the selling mortgagee did not describe in an advertisement for the property the correct nature of the planning permission, with the result that it was sold at an auction for a price below its true value. The sale did not realise the full amount owed to the mortgagee by the mortgagor. When the mortgagee claimed for the balance, the mortgagor claimed that they had not exercised a duty of care and sold the property at an undervalue.

HELD: The mortgagee had been negligent and was held liable to the mortgagor.
It can be seen from the decision in *Parker-Tweedale* v *Dunbar Bank plc and Others* [1990] that a mortgagee in exercising a power of sale over mortgaged property only owes a duty to the mortgagor and not to the beneficiary of the trust of which it had notice.
In *Bank of Cyprus (London) Ltd* v *Gill* [1980] it was held that the bank is under no obligation to wait to keep the business running pending sale or to delay a sale in an expectation in a rising property market.

13. *Deeley* v *Lloyds Bank Ltd* **[1912]**
The bank had advanced money to the customer against the security of a second mortgage and was held to have had notice of a third mortgage to its customer's sister. However, upon receipt of notice the bank failed to stop the account. As a result the subsequent credits totalled more than the customer's debt outstanding with the bank. Subsequently its customer was made bankrupt and the sale of the property by the bank realised a sum just sufficient to repay the first and second mortgages.
HELD: The third mortgagee, its customer's sister, had priority over fresh advances because the payments which were credited to the account after receipt of notice of the third mortgage wiped out the advance outstanding at the time of the notice. The third mortgagee was entitled to the sale proceeds after the first mortgage was repaid.

14. *Saunders* v *Anglia Building Society* [1971]

An elderly woman could not read the documents she was signing as her glasses were broken. She believed she was transferring her house to her nephew when in fact she was transferring it to another person. The liability was denied on the grounds that the transfer was void.

HELD: The mistake was due to lack of exercising reasonable care and therefore the claim could not succeed.

15. *Mackenzie* v *Royal Bank of Canada* [1934]

Mrs Mackenzie avoided her liability on a guarantee given to the bank to secure her husband's liability, because the bank misrepresented that the shares she had deposited earlier would be returned to her.

HELD: That the guarantee was unenforceable because of misrepresentation.

16. *Woolcott* v *Sun Alliance and London Insurance Ltd* [1978]

Woolcott completed an application form for a building society loan on a mortgage to purchase a house. The building society insured all the properties mortgaged to it under a block policy with the insurers. The application form required the applicants to disclose whether there were 'other matters which should be taken into account'. Woolcott did not make any disclosure regarding this question although he had served a long prison sentence for robbery. The house was damaged by fire. Although the insurers paid the building society the amount of their advance, they refused to pay Woolcott's claim because he had not disclosed his criminal record.

HELD: Woolcott's claim failed because he did not disclose the material fact regarding his criminal record. This information was material for disclosure since it would influence the judgment of an insurer.

17. *Spencer* v *Clarke* [1878]

A lender accepted an assignment of a policy as security which the borrower said he had left at home but would provide the following day. The lender gave notice of assignment to the insurance company. The policy was, in fact, deposited by the borrower with another lender as security for an earlier advance, notice of which was not given to the insurer of that prior charge.

HELD: The first mortgagee's claim had priority because the mortgagor's failure to produce the policy to the second lender constituted constructive notice of the prior charge. By giving express notice to the insurance company, the second lender could not reverse the priority. On the facts, the possession of the policy was more important than notice to the issuing company.

In *Newman* v *Newman* [1885] it was held that priority of assignment is determined by the date on which notice is received by the insurance company.

18. London Joint Stock Bank Ltd v Simmons [1892]

A stockbroker pledged bearer securities belonging to Simmons, a client, to secure his own overdraft. The bank was not aware whether or not the securities belonged to him and made no enquiries. The broker absconded and the bank realised the securities. Simmons sued the bank for their return claiming that the bank should have enquired into their ownership before accepting the pledge.

HELD: On the facts there were no suspicious circumstances involved in the transaction and the bank was therefore under no duty to make inquiries. The bank had acted in good faith and was entitled to retain and realise the securities.

19. Coleman v London County and Westminster Bank Ltd [1916]

The bank was unaware that its equitable charge over debenture stock was subject to a trust. The chargor held it on trust for other persons. When the bank became aware of the existence of this trust, it took a transfer of the debentures into its own name and registered them, thus becoming the proprietor under a legal charge. The beneficiaries brought an action to have the bank's charge set aside.

HELD: The beneficiaries were successful on the grounds that the bank was on notice of the prior equitable interest when it took its legal mortgage.

20. Sheffield Corporation v Barclay [1905]

Barclays Bank sent to the Corporation a transfer instrument signed by the two registered holders in favour of a Mr Barclay, as the nominee for Barclays Bank Ltd. One of the signatories of the transfer, whose signature was forged, brought an action against the Corporation which had to reimburse him with a new holding in the stock. The Corporation in turn looked to the bank which resisted the claim, but lost.

HELD: In forwarding the transfer for registration it had impliedly represented that the transfer was genuine and was therefore liable to indemnify the Corporation against the loss.

In *Yeung and Another* v *Hong Kong and Shanghai Banking Corporation* [1980] the stockbroker's action to claim relief on the principle outlined in

Sheffield Corporation v *Barclay* failed as it was held that the bank's failure to check the signature was not sufficient reason to prevent the bank from relying on the implied indemnity from the stockbrokers at the time of taking the transfer and when the stockbroker had impliedly represented that the signature was genuine.

21. *Re Yeovil Glove Co. Ltd* [1965]
Yeovil Glove Co. Ltd's overdraft was secured by a fixed charge over its factory. Later, when it was heavily in debt, the bank threatened to call up the debt unless the company provided original security. Yeovil Glove Co. Ltd gave security of a floating charge, but when the company could not repay its debts, the bank appointed a receiver. Liquidation took place within 12 months of the creation of the floating charge. During this period, payments made into the account exceeded the amount of the overdraft outstanding at the date of creation of the floating charge. The liquidator challenged the validity of this charge. The bank did not contend that the company was solvent on the date it gave the floating charge.

HELD: Because of the operation of rule in *Clayton's* case, subsequent credits in wiped out the original debt and subsequent payments out were considered as new advances and, by virtue of s.322 of the Companies Act 1948 (now s. 245, IA 1986), were fully covered by the floating charge.

22. *Victors Ltd* v *Lingard* [1927]
Victors Ltd's overdraft with Midland Bank was secured by the joint and several guarantee of the directors. Subsequently, the directors passed a resolution authorising the company to give a security of a debenture. Articles of Victors Ltd did not have a provision allowing the directors to vote on a matter in which they had a personal interest. Later, Victors Ltd went into liquidation and the liquidator contended that the security of debenture was invalid because the directors' resolution did not conform with the articles, and because the directors who had voted to grant a debenture would benefit.

HELD: The liquidator's claim succeeded on the grounds that the resolution was a nullity, but nevertheless the company could not deny its liability because by its subsequent dealings with the bank it had led the bank to believe the validity of the debenture.

23. *Siebe Gorman & Co. Ltd* v *Barclays Bank Ltd* [1979]
The company gave security of a debenture to its bank for its borrowings. The

debenture incorporated a clause whereby the company covenanted to pay all monies collected into its bank account, thus creating a fixed charge on future debts. Later the company acquired a bill of exchange. The problem arose in deciding whether the bank acquired an effective fixed charge which attached to the bill before its transfer and hence in priority to the rights of the transferee.

HELD: This created an effective fixed charge on debts but the bank's claim failed on other grounds.

24. *Aluminium Industrie Vaasen B.V. v Romalpa Aluminium Ltd* [1976]

A Dutch company (the plaintiff) was a supplier of aluminium foil to an English company. The supplier company, in their contract with the English company, had expressly reserved the title to the foil supplied, and included in the contract a clause whereby title to the foil would only pass to the buyer when he had been paid in full. The English company went into receivership after taking delivery of the foil but before paying for it. By that time the foil had been on-sold and the sale proceeds were paid to the administrative receiver. The plaintiff company claimed that they were entitled to those goods.

HELD: Until the payment for the goods was made, the supplier retained title to the goods and that resale took place by the buyer as an agent. Therefore the monies paid after resale of goods were held in trust for the supplier.

25. *Charterbridge Corporation Ltd v Lloyds Bank Ltd* [1969]

The question of commercial justification and *ultra vires* doctrine was considered in respect of the validity of inter-company guarantees. Charterbridge gave a guarantee supported by a legal charge for facilities to P Ltd (another company in the group). All the group companies had common directors and shareholders. The companies were trading as property developers, and Charterbridge's memorandum included a clause allowing the company to acquire properties for investment purposes with a limited power of realisation and also a power to give guarantees. The plaintiff claimed that the charge over supporting security was void because it had been created for purposes outside the scope of the company's business.

HELD: The transaction was for the benefit of the company giving the security and the plaintiff's action failed.

The concept of commercial justification was also considered in *Wallersteiner v Moir* [1974].

26.   *Royal British Bank* v *Turquand* [1856]

The directors of the company had power to issue bonds if authorised by a general resolution of the company. They issued bonds to the Royal British Bank without any such resolution.

HELD: The bank could sue on the bonds on the assumption that the resolution had been passed. It was not bound to enquire into the internal proceedings of the company, if it was satisfied that the proposed transaction was not inconsistent with the memorandum and articles.

27.   *Clough Mill Ltd* v *Martin* [1984]

A mill was a supplier of yarn for the manufacture of fabrics. The contract terms of Clough Mill stated that it would retain ownership until payment in full was received and if the yarn was to be admixed, the end product would form part of the supplier's property. The company's receiver claimed that the supply contract relating to the yarn was equivalent to a charge that was void against him for want of registration.

HELD: A charge can only be created as security on the property owned. As the buyer never owned the yarn and could not create charge over it to the supplier, registration was not required.

28.   *Re M. Kushler Ltd* [1943]

One of the directors of this company gave security of his guarantee for his company's borrowing. When the two directors (husband and wife) realised that the company was insolvent, they arranged receipts from trade debtors to be paid into the company's account but did not pay the trade creditors. Before the company went into a creditors' voluntary liquidation, the overdraft was paid off.

HELD: The bank preferred the guarantor and the payments to the bank amounted to fraudulent preference as the cash was paid into the company's bank account to reduce the directors' liability as guarantor. The bank was asked to return the monies. The decision was confirmed in *Liquidator of West Mercia Safety Wear Ltd* v *Dodd* [1988].

29.   *Re Grays Inn Construction Co. Ltd* [1980]

Between the date of presentation of petition (3 August 1972) and the date of the order for compulsory winding up (9 October 1972), the bank account of the company was overdrawn. Between 3 August and 9 October the bank allowed operation of the account whereby £25,313 was paid in and £24,129 drawn out. The bank relied on a guarantee supported by security given by the managing director. The bank had actual notice of the petition on 17 August although it was advertised on 10 August. When the liquidator claimed against the bank the amount of £24,129 drawn out of the account, the bank argued that it had allowed the company to operate its account to enable it to carry on its business.

HELD: The bank had actual notice of the petition on 17 August and must therefore refund all monies paid from the account after that date. The court, as an exception, allowed payments up to 17 August under s. 127 from the account after the presentation of the petition, without drawing any distinction between payments to the company and payments to third parties.

30. Re William Hall (Contractors) Ltd [1967]

The company borrowed from the bank against mortgages of company properties as security. The company owed to the bank £2,274 advanced for wages (preferential debt) and £5,647 (non-preferential debt), totalling £7,921. The bank applied £5,779, received from the realisation of the security to clear the non-preferential debt and the balance was applied to clear the preferential debts. In respect of the balance of £2,142 the bank then proved as a preferential creditor.

HELD: The court upheld this procedure and confirmed that a secured creditor is entitled to apply the realisation proceeds of its security to clear whichever liability of the debtor he chooses.

31. Barclays Bank plc v O'Brien [1993]

The decision in this case provided guidelines for taking of third party security, which lenders should apply in all cases where there is a risk that the transaction can be set aside as against the principal debtor on the grounds of undue influence, or misrepresentation.

In this case Barclays Bank took a legal charge over Mr and Mrs O'Brien's matrimonial home to secure Mr O'Brien's business indebtedness. The branch, where the documents were sent for execution by Mr and Mrs O'Brien, failed to explain the terms and effect of the charge or recommend independent legal advice to them. Without reading the terms of the charge, Mrs O'Brien relied on her husband's false representation that the charge was limited to £60,000 only and would be released in three weeks. The charge was, in fact, in the standard clearing bank form for 'all monies' and without time limitation. The bank sought to enforce the charge when Mr O'Brien's business overdraft

189

exceeded £154,000. Mrs O'Brien claimed that she was induced to execute the legal charge by the misrepresentation of her husband.

HELD: The Court of Appeal held that the charge was only enforceable by the bank against Mrs O'Brien to the extent of £60,000, the amount which Mrs O'Brien had understood she had agreed to secure. Lord Justice Scott further added that, when taking security from married women for their husband's debts, creditors should take reasonable steps to ensure that (i) their consent was not obtained by the husband's undue influence or misrepresentation; and (ii) they understood the nature and effect of the transaction they were entering into.

The House of Lords dismissed the suggestion that third-party security given by a wife could not be set aside simply on the ground that the wife did not fully understand the nature and effect of the transaction. They added that the lenders will not be able to enforce the security if they had actual or constructive notice of the facts giving rise to the wife's equitable right to set aside the transaction against the husband (if he had exerted undue influence or misrepresented the facts). Their Lordships held that, in view of the emotional bond of trust and confidence between husband and wife, a creditor will be on constructive notice when accepting security from a wife offering to stand as surety for her husband's debts. Reasonable steps should have been taken to satisfy that the wife's agreement to stand as surety had been properly obtained.

It was held that the same principles would apply to all other cases where there was an emotional relationship between co-habitees, where the creditor is similarly on inquiry whenever he is aware that the surety 'places trust and confidence in the principal debtor in relation to his financial affairs'. The above test can equally apply to other relationships, e.g. parent/child, etc.

32.   *Re Telomatic Ltd, Barclays Bank plc* v *Cyprus Popular Bank Ltd* [1993]
Barclays Bank plc took a legal charge dated 4 January 1989 from Telomatic to secure its loan. Although Barclays registered the charge at the Land Registry, it omitted to register it at Companies Registry. Barclays realised later in the year that it had failed to register the charge. In October 1990, Cyprus Popular Bank Ltd took a second charge over the property in question. Barclays made an application to the Companies Registry, to register out of time and sought an order removing the proviso that it be without prejudice to the rights acquired by other creditors between the date of creation of the charge and the date of its actual registration, or modifying to exclude Cyprus Popular Bank's priority.

HELD: Barclays made three attempts to obtain a valid charge, but the court refused registration out of time on the grounds that:

(a)   Barclays had not provided any evidence as to the circumstances in which its charge had not been registered.

(b)   The court was neither advised of any reason for not registering the charge nor informed of other grounds to justify late registration.

(c)   Since failure to register might have prejudiced other creditors and no case was made on the evidence that it had not done so, the court's discretion to extend time under s. 404 of the Companies Act 1985 did not arise, especially due to the delay in lodging the application and attempting to rectify the situation without applying to court by taking further charges.

(d)   It was further held that even if the order would have been made allowing late registration, it would have been subject to the proviso protecting the rights acquired by the secured creditors before the actual registration.

33.   *CIBC Mortgages plc* v *Pitt and Another* [1993]

In 1986 Mrs Pitt, unwillingly at first, agreed under her husband's pressure to sign a joint application which stated the purpose of the loan was for the purchase of a holiday home. Against a legal charge on the matrimonial home a loan of £150,000 by way of remortgage was given to the couple. The husband used the money to invest in shares on the stock market. These shares were then pledged by Mr Pitt, as further security for further loans before the 1987 stock market crash. The bank called in the loan and security. Mrs Pitt defended her action, on the ground of undue influence and misrepresentation, and claimed that the bank had not explained to her the terms of the documents she was signing.

HELD: The House of Lords in this case held that if a wife was induced by the undue influence of her husband to charge the matrimonial home as security of a joint loan to husband and wife, the lender would not be affected by the undue influence if the husband was not acting as an agent for the bank for procuring the wife's agreement, and had no actual or constructive notice of the undue influence. It was held that a claim to set aside a transaction on the grounds of undue influence, whether presumed or actual, could not succeed unless it could be proved that the impugned transaction was manifestly disadvantageous to the claimant.

The House of Lords said that the decision in this case reaffirmed the law laid down in *National Westminster Bank plc* v *Morgan* [1985], and as interpreted by the Court of Appeal in *Bank of Credit and Commerce International SA* v *Aboody* [1989].

191

Index